everything you need to know for a

Cassette
Ministry

everything you need to know for a

Cassette Ministry

Cassettes in the Context of a Total Christian Communication Program

BY
VIGGO B. SØGAARD

BETHANY FELLOWSHIP, INC.
Minneapolis, Minnesota

Copyright © 1975
Bethany Fellowship, Inc.
All rights reserved

Published by Bethany Fellowship, Inc.
6820 Auto Club Road, Minneapolis, Minnesota 55438

Printed in the United States of America

Library of Congress Cataloging in Publication Data:

Søgaard, Viggo B, 1939-
   Everything you need to know for a cassette ministry.

    1. Phonotapes in church work.   I. Title.
BV652.83.S63   266'.0028   74-20915
ISBN 0-87123-125-5

Foreword

When Viggo Søgaard says that "people simply do not want to waste time reading," he is talking about the majority of people in this world, not some small fragment. No matter how fond of reading some of us may be, communicating with people is a matter of reaching out to where they are and accepting them in the way they are. That means, for the church, resisting the temptation to make literacy a requirement for salvation and spiritual development.

Not many years ago "missionary communication" meant a two-way wireless and a ritualistic round trip to the post office. Communication was concerned with a missionary's keeping in touch with "the outside world," and being able to get help for the expected emergencies. What a difference today! Communication is what the mission of the church is all about.

The technologies of communication have provided new approaches for outreach, beginning with field-based printing presses, then mass radio and the more specialized forms of audio—sound trucks, record distribution, and so forth. Now and then a motion picture, here and there a television production—missions follows not far behind the highly promoted approaches to communication in the secular world. Fine! And not so fine.

Especially in the field of mass communication, the church tends to copy without improving on the secular originals. So many gospel telecasts are warmed-over Welk; so many broadcasts are loyal continuations of early-day Revival Hour (modeled on long-forgotten "Uncle Ed" sort of primitive radio). Especially in missionary situations,

5

mass communication often is long on mass but short on communication.

The importance of communication is more than a matter of costly equipment and zingy gimmicks. Applied communication theory is the real frontier. Communication theory is becoming quite solid and dependable, thanks to the research that huge secular investments have enabled. Applying the findings of this research for the mission of the church takes responsible know-how.

The work of Viggo Søgaard is strong in applied theory. He and his colleagues in Thailand make the media work for them. Their projects are carefully grounded on the biblical foundations of responsible church outreach. And at the same time, their procedures and techniques are drawn from applied communication theory. Thus it follows that in giving us this book, Søgaard is concerned with far more than the techniques of mission outreach through cassettes; he takes us on a guided tour through the theory underlying his interesting and important radio and cassette ministries in Northern Thailand. As founder and director of the program, Søgaard has much to tell us. We read with interest, because this is substantial material, not idle speculations. For those who are involved in cassette ministries, it is especially useful to get this behind-the-scenes look at one of the more comprehensive cross-cultural communication systems serving the church of Jesus Christ. How important to see the particular roles that cassette recordings play—not the whole system, by any means!

Some of Søgaard's advice is based on the particular circumstances in Thailand. It would be superficial to transfer all the guidelines of the Thailand-targeted program to situations that are inherently different. And this is the ultimate importance of theory: it helps us get under the particulars to see *why* they work and thus make better transfers and translations to other situations.

As one who has been wrestling with the issue of literacy and its relationship to learning, I am delighted to find Søgaard sounding the call for rethinking the place of literacy in missions. Pragmatically, the problem is that so few non-literate people see the value of learning to read and write. (After all, when a whole society is organized around aural communication, print media can seem to be unimportant!) At a deeper level, the issue is to decide at what point and for what purposes literacy will be seen

6

as important *by the learners*, and to use non-literacy-based procedures up until that point.

Aware of the importance (and reverence?) that is given to print media by many within the church, Søgaard says, "Literature was the medium chosen by God to record His dealings with men. It started with God himself writing ... with His own fingers...." I would less generously force the question: what about the much older dependency on oral traditions: folk lore, fables, proverbs, traditional songs, and oral history? Consider the probability that some of the major biblical characters were illiterate! From our snug and smug posture in the "have" nations, it is so easy to see missions as dealing with the "have-not" nations—and to extend this faulty view to the matter of literacy. People are not more intelligent after they learn to read; illiteracy does not mean unreachable, stupid primitives. In certain societies, in fact, the skills of aural learning are more highly developed than we can imagine. We should learn to "connect" with these learning skills before we push the new learning skills that literacy demands. The outreach of the church is concerned with the message of good news—and that good news is Christ, not literacy.

Viggo Søgaard has provided this review of his work as a part of his year of graduate studies in the United States. One of the marks of a worthy graduate school is that it brings together people who have valuable knowledge and experiences to share with each other. In this sense, Søgaard has been a valuable graduate student in the worthy graduate school of Wheaton College. For all of this we can be grateful.

Read on! And help yourself to a tasty portion of communication theory, well seasoned by illustrations from a lively program of cassettes for reaching, winning, and teaching.

Ted Ward
Professor of Curriculum Research
Institute for International Studies
Michigan State University

Table of Contents

Introduction

The first request to write a cassette manual for Christian workers, and for foreign missionaries in particular, came less than two years after the first cassette player was put to use. With another two years to complete the task, the result is this book. The cassette was a new medium in Christian work, a medium that showed tremendous potentials. Yet to write a manual that could be used worldwide needed detailed research, study, and experimentation. If a truly comprehensive book were to be written, a volume several times the present size would be needed. This could be an important factor that would diminish and influence the use of the manual.

Selection of material has been based not only on personal experience, but also on the type of requests for help received from various parts of the world. A survey among missionaries also gave good indication of what is needed.

One missionary wrote, "We had talked about the format of material that is being put on cassettes. Could you elaborate some on that? I remember that you mentioned the use of scripted material instead of straight lectures. What length of cassettes have you found the most serviceable? Which are the easiest to program for? Which are the most effective to use, in your opinion? Have you continued to be pleased with the Philips cassettophones? What maintenance problems have you had with the units? Have any of these difficulties been hard to solve or eliminate?"

Another missionary wrote, "When I first started cassetting, I got jams of all sorts, and it has taken a long time to understand what is going wrong—I don't know for sure even now."

As a manual, this book should be read and used chapter by chapter. To understand and apply its implications, a thorough understanding of the first four chapters will be needed. When working on the material, no clear frame of reference was found, so the principles developed and explained in chapter two are used as the basis of our strategy and programming. These same principles can form the basis for any missionary strategy and any communications media used.

Technology has made fantastic progress since World War II. The main reason for this progress has been a tiny thing—the transistor. Transistors have caused technological miracles and produced complete new industries. Refined transistor techniques together with tape recording refinements introduced many possibilities for the present cassettes and cassette players—already refined industries. A short history with an amazing result. An overview of a cassette ministry is in chapter one.

As you begin, or continue, your cassette ministry, remember that this book is not the only one that suggests research as the foundation for strategy and planning. The Bible also says something on the subject,

> "Any enterprise is built by wise planning, becomes strong through common sense, and profits wonderfully by keeping abreast of the facts" (Prov. 24:34, Living Bible).

Many people deserve credit for help in making the cassette ministry work, especially the staff at Voice of Peace studios, Box 131, Chiang Mai, Thailand, and both Thai and missionaries. Professors in the Communications Department of Wheaton Graduate School have also been a great help and encouragement.

CHAPTER 1

The Cassette at Work

The third-term missionary had experienced many days like this before, but he never grew accustomed to the hot, tropical sun burning uncompassionately all day. As usual it had been a long, tedious journey on the dusty road. The young missionary, however, was more excited about this new experience. Though both were tired, they knew that a little group of relatively new believers in the village were waiting eagerly to listen to them and fellowship with them several hours that evening. From past experience, the older missionary knew that these isolated Christians liked to sing and would want to learn new hymns. This was going to take time and patience.

But how mistaken he was! He could hardly believe what he heard. These new Christians were singing hymns and knew most of them by heart. The secret? A small tape-recorder which another missionary had left in the village. The tremendous need had caused people to work on a solution to the teaching aspect of missionary work. But although the taperecorder was quite good, it was not the answer, for it was too costly and too complicated to operate.

The tapes in these earlier experiments carried the material that the first cassettes would carry a year later. By the vision and guidance given by God, work had begun on the cassette project from the Voice of Peace studios in Chiang Mai, North Thailand, long before the equipment was ready. Others were working too. Leslie Brierley of the International Survey Department in London mentioned that, for him, it was a 14-year-old vision being fulfilled in the cassette project unfolding first in Thailand and later in other countries. Different Christian organizations were also working to solve the problem. This need, the long years of preparation and the expectation of those involved were probably the reasons for the immediate use of cassettes and cassette-players after they became available.

Probably no other new tool used in Christian communication has enjoyed such an enthusiastic acceptance as the audio-cassette did. The first players went out from the Voice of Peace in June, 1969. Initial plans called for the use of about 12 cassette-players in a testing program covering 6 to 12 months. Within six months 90 cassette-players were in use; and within a year, more than 300. In less than 3 years over 1000 players had passed through Voice of Peace, and thousands of cassettes had been produced. They had gone to missionaries, churches, and national workers. The impact of these small, humble tools was felt almost immediately.

For example, a Dutch missionary working near the Laos border in East Thailand had experienced the Lord's blessing on his work. Suddenly he found himself the only minister for at least 25 small groups of new Christians. The area was large. It was rough spiritually, and some Christians were being persecuted. It was also rough traveling, for the roads were few and bad. Some places were 50 miles away. How could he effectively teach these new Christians the Word of God? There was seemingly no answer. Then cassettes came along and, by the help of Christian friends, cassettes and cassette-players were purchased. His ministry was instantly changed. Now he could visit a group of believers, leave the cassette with them, and know they would receive good teaching while he was away. He would still return regularly and have fellowship with them. What a difference!

A handful of new Christians in a faraway village was one place where he left a cassette-player. Within three months they had won twenty others for Christ, and in less than a year a strong church had been established in that village—a church that was even able to withstand an attack from false teachers.

Take another example of a cassette-player that brought blessing to an inaccessible district. Just two months earlier it had arrived in Mr. Beng's house. Mr. Beng was paralyzed in a shooting incident four years earlier, but had recently accepted the Lord. His experience of salvation in Jesus Christ filled him with the only real joy he had ever known. But he longed for an outlet for his new-found faith. Then the missionary provided Beng with the tool that helped him to witness and grow in the knowledge of the Lord. He listened all day to the cassette-player and sometimes at night, too, when his sores kept him awake. But what an amazing growth in grace—just through listening to cassettes expounding God's Word. In two short months Beng had won nine others to Jesus Christ. A simple cassette with a helpless man made all the difference. What busy missionary could have given Mr. Beng even a fraction of this time? And what missionary would have had the patience and wisdom to repeat his message 30 times until even Mr. Beng had learned it?

Or take the example of Mr. Tap, a village headman. In his five years as a Christian, he didn't pray in worship meetings and didn't witness. He was too timid, or afraid he wouldn't say it the proper way. Then he received a cassette-player which he used during the missionary's furlough. After one year the missionary returned. He was amazed at what he saw. Not only did Mr. Tap lead the meeting at his own house, but he prayed and read the Bible. He was a changed man. Repeated listening—perhaps 50 times in that year—had solved Mr. Tap's learning problem and had built up his confidence to speak for his Lord. Once again a simple cassette became a teacher where no other teacher was available. It persisted where human teachers would have given up.

Repetition is one of the fundamental principles of the learning process. Like Mr. Tap, many others also were able to learn because of this great advantage. The cassette has many other advantages, too, which are not matched by any other communication tool. It is small, easy to handle, and hours of programming can be carried in your pocket. Cassette-players are so easy to operate that even the most illiterate, primitive man can learn to use it. There is no tape to thread and no tone-arm to scratch.

Some of these advantages were factors that made the difference for Boon, a Christian who lived in East Thailand. Fifteen difficult years had passed by, years in which he faced opposition. His wife, a leader in the local religious association, did all she could to make life miserable for him. Her anger blazed especially when friends visited Boon. Like one possessed, she made as much noise as she could so that the visitors could not pray or have fellowship together. Only the grace of God in Boon's heart helped him to endure these long years. But Boon's faith did not fail. He prayed constantly for his wife's salvation.

Then a strange thing happened. A missionary friend asked Boon if he would like to borrow a cassette-player (also called a cassettophone). What amazed Boon was that his wife allowed him to listen—if he kept the volume down. Then one day as he listened, he discovered his wife was listening as well. He turned the volume up a little. She didn't object. Later he turned it up a bit more. After a while he played the cassette-player at full volume, even the neighbors could listen. Recent news was that Boon's wife went to church three times and was on the verge of believing. A simple cassette had smashed barriers that people alone could not overcome in 15 years.

In the beginning, most cassettes were made as a basic Bible teaching series. This was where the main need was seen, and so efforts were concentrated there. Experience showed that effective evangelism must have a big portion of Bible teaching to bring about a lasting fruit. By repeated listening, basic truths of the Word of God were understood and grasped, the new Christian understood what he had done, and he was eager to witness to others.

In a country with a high illiteracy rate cassettes make the difference. For example, a Thai Christian regularly took his cassette-player to a friend's house. Some neighbors often came in to listen, too, and after a time three of them accepted Christ as their Savior. They said later, "We heard about Christ before, and we read tracts, but we did not understand the Gospel until now." The cassette had broken through literacy barriers.

Not all cassettes had Bible teaching, however. New Christians wanted to learn to sing—sing the tunes right, the same way Christians were singing them in other churches. By far the most popular cassettes have been those with Thai music and Thai tunes. One missionary, a gifted music teacher, wrote, "The machines do more in one week than I can do in months." By using cassette-players new Christians learn to sing right away to the correct tunes. What an improvement this makes in our church singing!

Music on cassettes also attracts other people. One Thai evangelist traveling by train played some Christian hymns. Soon three men sat close to him to enjoy the singing. Then the evangelist stopped the player and talked to the men for three hours about what it means to believe in Christ.

Cassettes are so handy that they can be taken anywhere, and will work everywhere—indoors and outdoors; at the beach, in the hotel; in the sun and in rain; in automobiles, on trains, and even on the back of a buffalo; they can be carried upside down, swung, shaken, and dropped, and still continue playing while going through this sort of treatment! Though there is a limit to how much abuse they can stand, they are in fact marvelous, versatile tools for the Christian worker, and for many, many others.

It is a great thrill to see how a cassette-player may be used to deepen the lives of Christians. Many of them have been professing Christians for years, but have rarely witnessed for Christ. Others—perhaps naturally shy, they lack education, or for other reasons—are quiet Christians. But put a cassette-player in their hands and they get turned on to witnessing.

One man in Maesod had been a Christian for two years. Extreme shyness kept him from even smiling at others. Then he borrowed a cassette-player and played it every day at full volume. In a short time his life changed, for he won two neighbors to the Lord and opened up a new village to the Gospel. A cassette made the difference.

The story of Nai Ae is thrilling too. Many years ago he came to Thailand from Burma. Though he married a Thai wife, he never learned to read or write Thai, and his grasp of spoken Thai was limited. Through listening to the Voice of Peace radio ministry every morning, he experienced the reality of the Gospel. Later he received a cassette-player and used it whenever possible. He learned hymns and sang along with the cassette. His wife listened and she, too, became a Christian. Both of them testified that until they received the cassette and were able to hear the message again and again, they never really understood it.

Nai Ae took the cassette-player to relatives and friends

who lived in the surrounding mountain villages. Some were converted. Finally he began gathering these new believers on Sundays for a service. The cassette-player was the preacher! This was just the right tool for him, as it has proven to be for many others also.

Mr. Pun had been an elder in an old established church for a number of years, but he found it difficult to witness to others. Then one day he borrowed a cassette-player for a month so he could take it to a village where some of his relatives lived. With this new helper he found it quite easy to begin testifying. He soon began going to three other villages as well. Even when he gave the cassette-player back, his ministry continued. He had memorized much from the cassettes, and it had given him confidence. Within a few months several families in three of these villages were trusting the Lord. A worker had received a tool that he could use!

It should be stressed here that although the cassette-player is very useful, it is merely a machine. While it does a lot in absence of people, it will never take the place of the missionary or the local Christian. It is just a tool—like giving a carpenter a hammer, or the electrician a screwdriver. The cassette does not take the man's place, but it helps him accomplish more with greater effectiveness. The leader of one of the largest missionary societies in Thailand wrote, "Cassette-players have greatly increased the effectiveness of our missionary force. Our folk are amazed at the results they bring."

A doctor at a Christian hospital was asked about the use of cassette-players at the hospital. He answered, "They are terrific. They are in use constantly." As a result of that doctor's recommendation, a big order for cassettes was sent to the Voice of Peace in Chiang Mai.

One of the encouraging aspects of the cassette project is the interest Christians at home take in the project. One man wrote about the cassette-players to his home church's youth group. After reading the letter in the youth meeting, the group leader suggested that they should have a part in this work, so they decided to take an offering to buy one cassette-player. To their surprise they received enough money to buy six cassette-players.

Another missionary, who works among tribal people in North Thailand, described in a letter the great usefulness of cassette-players in his tribal work. A friend who pastored a large church mentioned to his congregation that he would be glad to receive offerings from anyone who wished to give $25 for a cassette-player for use in North Thailand. About one hundred people responded that same morning and, as a result, 100 cassette-players are in use among tribal people scattered in the North of Thailand.

In a number of cases, local Christians who can afford it have bought a cassette-player themselves, or a church will buy one or two players for use in their evangelistic witness. Usually, however, people are too poor to buy them personally. After all, $25 for a player and $2 to $3 for each cassette (including high custom duty to pay in Thailand) is just too much for a poor man. In most cases missionaries, or their missions, have bought the cassette-players and lent them out. One American organization provided funds for 100 cassette-players to be used in the area where an interdenominational mission is working. But the demand for players always exceeds the supply, since almost daily requests for more players come in. At this crucial time, Thailand could use thousands of cassette-players—not to mention the other countries in South East Asia.

A cassette project needs financing, not only for cassettes and players, but for the production equipment and the high cost of production. Fortunately, Voice of Peace is also engaged in an extensive radio ministry and other types of mass media, so studios and production facilities for the master tapes are available. One main need at one time was for a high-speed cassette duplicator. Part of the money for this expensive piece of equipment was graciously provided by another organization who wanted to give encouragement in the work. The major part of the remaining part came from a person in Switzerland, whom we didn't know. But it came at the right time when it was needed. Very clearly God's hand was at work in this particular ministry, which has helped to lead hundreds of people to Christ, to build new churches, and to train Christians to become effective witnesses.

This leads to another point which should be stressed, and that is that the work is a spiritual work and therefore needs prayer. Prayer is needed for Christians as they use the cassette-players in their districts. Prayer is needed for those at Voice of Peace who make the cassette programs and record the cassettes. Prayer is needed for a great harvest.

Special programming for cassettes is important, and this is the purpose of this book. Each need or ministry requires different types of cassette programs. An example is the Cassette Bible School for training lay leaders. Many Christians who are potential leaders in the churches cannot possibly go to a Bible school, so a method is being developed by which the Bible school will come to them in their own homes. The course features a Thai teacher and two students. Questions of interest in the study are drawn out in a dialog between the teacher and students. In this way the student at home can identify himself with those on the cassette and study right along with them. Printed material is also given to the student with a list of questions to answer. It is believed that tremendous changes in the church will result from this course.

Take, for example, the group of faithful elders in a leprosy church. They are not able to go to Bible school, even though they have to preach each Sunday. Now the Bible school has come to them, and they eagerly study the material.

Interest in the Cassette Bible School came from all over Thailand. This response underlined the tremendous need there is for an extension teaching aimed at lay leaders—a program especially suited for the Thai. The cassettes again seemed to be the part that made it possible. In one church, many gathered the first evening with the Cassette Bible School material to study. They stayed up until 2 a.m. before they finally went to bed.

Many more stories could be told, but use your own imagination and faith. As you imagine more than 1600 cassette-players teaching, preaching, and singing as they win others to Christ across Thailand, try also to imagine what they can do for you in your ministry. The remainder of this book is an attempt to share what has been learned so far, so that you too will be able to use this amazing cassette effectively in your outreach for Christ.

CHAPTER 2

The Basic Principles
and Theory

The place of the cassette ministry in a total communications program can be determined only after a close analysis of the environment and of the media. For such an analysis to be helpful and valid, it must be based on clearly defined theories and principles.

THE COMMISSION TO COMMUNICATE

The Great Commission, the task of communicating the Gospel that was given to the disciples, was not intended for them alone. It was a missionary command to the Church and to its individual members. The very essence and nature and doctrine of Christianity has missionary emphasis and thrust built right into it, but by specifically stating the command, our Lord sharply focused on the missionary responsibility of the Church. How well the Church has lived up to this commission of the Lord—or failed to live up to it—is clearly evident in the world today. The great majority of the earth's population have yet to accept Jesus Christ as Lord and Savior. The task ahead in missions is a vast but wonderful one, and any result causes joy in heaven and on earth.

The Great Commission

The Great Commission was a composite commission. We find it recorded in all four Gospels, though each one emphasizes certain aspects of the commission.

1. *It was a commission to evangelize.* "Go ye into all the world and preach the Gospel to all creation." [1]

2. *It was a commission to make disciples.* "Make disciples in all the nations." [2]

3. *It was a commission to teach.* "Teach these new disciples to obey all the commands I have given you." [3] These basic aspects of the Great Commission never change, and time and culture have no influence on them.

There are also some other basic aspects of the missionary task that should always be kept in mind, and be fundamental to all our missionary thinking and endeavor.

1. *Missionary work must be a spiritual work.* In all missionary work we can never emphasize too strongly that the task is one in which, ultimately, all results will depend on the Holy Spirit. But in the task of proclaiming the Gospel, the Spirit utilizes the Church and her missionaries as His agents.

2. *Missionary work must be based on the Word of God.* The essential context and content of all the aspects of the Great Commission is Bible teaching, and that centers around Jesus Christ.

3. *Missionary work must be carried out in faith.* Christianity is a religion of faith. It is through the eyes of faith that man beholds God; and without faith, no spiritual work can be carried out. Salvation is received by faith, Christian life is lived in and by faith, and believing the implications of the Gospel for all mankind, the missionary task is accepted in faith.[4]

As Christians we have a religion and a message that is different from all others. This message is relevant at all times for all people.

In addition to these great, unchanging aspects of the Great Commission, there is still another. The human aspect is involved in the execution of the commission. Man lives in time, society, and culture; and as times and cultures change, so do the ways in which man acts and communicates. This demands much from the Christian communicator. Christ knew this,[5] and Paul tried always to be "all things to all men." [6]

24

In order to be effective—and accountable—in their Christian communication, modern Christian and missionary organizations are taking increasing advantage of advanced, scientific management tools in the form of research, strategy and planning. Such procedures have not been without criticism, though. Some people consider it the work of man as opposed to the work and guidance of the Holy Spirit. It cannot be denied that the Scriptures often stress the need to rely on the Spirit. The teaching of Jesus in John's Gospel is an example, and the incident with Philip in Acts 8 seems to be in complete opposition to marketing and management principles. It is pointed out that, in many instances, Paul was led by the Spirit to do certain things, or go to certain places.[7]

On the other hand, Scripture also gives many examples of the use of management and leadership. Jesus himself is an example by the way He chose His disciples, taught them by association and demonstration, and supervised and delegated work. The story of Joseph also illustrates the magnificent use of management, as does the story of Moses. In Acts 6 we see a selection of administrators to care for the church's food distribution program.

The question for us is not, what side should we be on? Rather, we must accept both sides. The reason for many controversies has been the lack of definition of terms; this has also been the case with 'management.' The term is used here as implying all aspects of management, but it can be used almost interchangeably with 'leadership,' another term accepted everywhere in the Church. Christian management is leadership, i.e., it is stewardship over the talents of others, getting things done through other people.[8]

As mentioned above, Paul "became all things to all men." When speaking in the synagogue, his message was designed for the Jews; but when he was speaking in Athens, his message was designed for the Gentiles. It is necessary that we today have leaders who "understand the times and know what Israel ought to do."[9] It is necessary that we have managers who are able, under God, to recognize each man's gifts, so that the full force and capacity of the 'body' can be put to work. The great tools that can help management to be effective in communicating the Gospel today are the modern methods of research and analysis.

The principles set forth in this chapter are written in human terms, but underneath, above, within, and around we must depend on the Holy Spirit. Prayer must certainly be an integral part of our ministry.

The Principles of a Total Program

In discussing the advantages and disadvantages of various communicaton media, or the relative strengths of one method as compared to another, often the discussion is carried on without any clear frame of reference. One man may say he can win more people for Christ in one week by personal evangelism than a radio station can do in a whole year. On the other hand, the broadcaster talks about the millions he is reaching. Both may be partly right, but they are wrong in their assumptions. The main question is, how and for what purpose is each media being used? And, is it according to the inherent and obvious advantages of that particular media or method in that particular situation?

A carpenter does have a wide variety of tools, each one designed for certain specific purposes. When building a house, he may use all his tools, but each one is for a different purpose depending on what part of the work he is doing. They all help him to lay the foundation, build the house, and complete it by the final touches of the paint brush. So it is with the process of leading a man to Christ. The media or method that is used to bring about the final commitment of a person is not necessarily more successful than the media that started the process.

We should never, for example, expect that Christian radio can accomplish the whole task. Neither should radio broadcasting be even considered exclusively, unless, of course, no other approach is available. The same is the case for a piece of "reaping" literature produced for the Western audience. We cannot expect it to accomplish the same task among people in the Orient. In most cases a multi-media approach, together with interpersonal contacts, would be the ideal strategy. Effective planners will not begin by asking how we can use a particular media, or tract, or radio program that is dear to us; but, rather, what is the need and task that must be met and accomplished? Then must follow a search for the right media and program to accomplish the job.

A large proportion of Christian work and use of media has centered around very limited areas of the total program that it needed to carry out. On many mission fields, tasks were often left undone, and the translated western "evangelistic" material was far too narrow in scope to reach the intended audience.

There has been a need for some clear frame of reference by which one could explain the integration of various media, indicate unreached areas, and guide the development of new projects, like a cassette project, designed to meet these areas. The need called for an overall conceptual model by which to design and explain the various parts of the total program needed to fulfill the Great Commission. The Spiritual Segmentation Model, which is explained on the following pages, was developed for this purpose.

Spiritual Segmentation for the Total Program

Basic Segmentation Model

In order to fulfill the Great Commission, we must have a total program that is designed to cover all aspects of the task. As was seen earlier, the Commission is to preach the Gospel to all men, make disciples from all nations, and teach them. This gives us three distinct areas to which we shall designate the more popular terms of: sowing, reaping and refining. The basic segmentation model, shown on figure 1, makes this task visible.

Spiritual Position of Man on the Segmentation Model

Each person is somewhere on the line between A and Z. A is the man who knows absolutely nothing about Christianity, and Z is the fully trained Christian leader. Our purpose is, therefore, to lead a man from where he is now on toward Z; and, in order to do that, we need a total program that covers all sections between A and Z. Too often some vital links have been missing. Perhaps the work has centered around reaping when no effective sowing has been done, or sowing only with little attempt to reap.

In between A and Z there are all the conceivable stages in understanding and Christian maturity. Some of these stages are indicated on figure 2. The basic need for the missionary or Christian worker is to know where on the

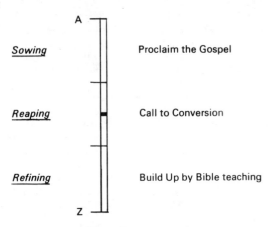

Figure 1
Basic Model for Spiritual Segmentation

model his audience is; that is, which segment is he trying to reach? and, which media is effective for that particular ministry? A message designed for one audience segment will generally not be effective for another segment. This means also that it cannot be expected that the person who is at point B on the model can be expected to respond to material designed for the person who is at point J.

Reach of Evangelistic Material Published in the West

Recent research clearly confirms this principle. One piece of evangelistic material was published in the United States, and it was designed for the higher educated classes who had at least a Christian cultural background. This material was in turn translated into a number of other languages, where it was supposed to do the same job as it had done in the U.S. Tests showed that it would work the same way in the translated edition with the same kind of audience, but the problem was that the audience who spoke that language was at a different stage on the model. It seems as if this is the case for most evangelistic material published in the West. It is intended for people who are somewhere past G on the model, while the majority of the population in the orient will be between A and D. (See figure 3.)

28

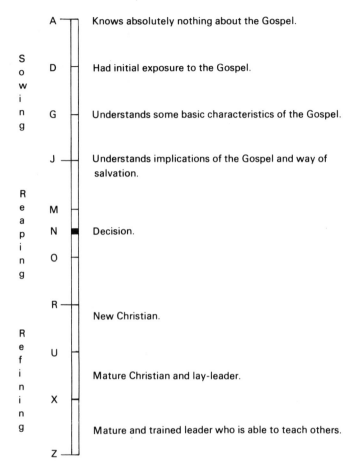

Figure 2
The Spiritual Position of Man As
Explained on the Segmentation Model

The parable of the Sower seems to indicate this same principle. It was the person who understood and received that in turn bore much fruit. If we aim at decisions without understanding, we will most likely see a repetition of the parable of the Sower, in that, the seed will fall on the first three kinds of soil.

The Program Components of the
Three Major Stages of the Task

When discussing the use of Christian radio, cassettes, or other media—and, in particular, programming for the media—it is necessary to further identify various program components involved at each stage of the task as shown on the model. With an understanding of the limitations of individual programs, a clear definition of purpose is needed to establish exact goals for individual programs.

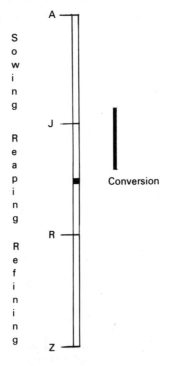

Figure 3

Effective, but not necessarily intended, reach of most 'evangelistic material' published in the West.

Sowing involves: Bible teaching, awareness of the Gospel, acceptability and relevancy of the Gospel.

Reaping involves: Bible teaching and counseling—a general calling to the Lord.

Refining involves: Bible teaching, religious news, devotions and fellowship, missions and general outreach, stewardship.

This is indicated on figure 4, but it should of course be remembered that several different segments exist within each of the three major segments. For effective programming each segment needs to be identified.

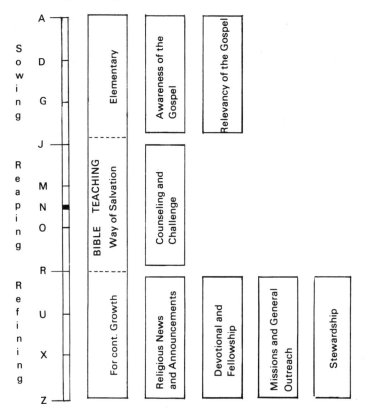

Figure 4
Program Components

31

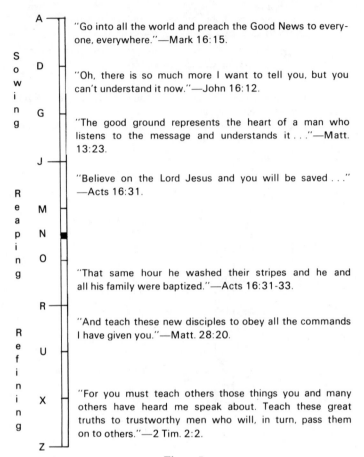

Figure 5
Some Scriptural Verses Supporting the Total Program Principle

THE COMMUNICATION PROCESS

Ever since man was created, God has attempted to communicate with him in one way or another—directly to his heart, by visions, by the prophets, through the Word, and conclusively, by His Son who through the incarnation became the full communication of God to man. God has also given man five senses through which he contacts society and his surroundings. They are: vision, hearing, feeling, smelling and tasting. All of these are "highways" to the mind, highways on which he transports or communicates his messages. Man also uses various communication media, which, in a sense, are 'extensions of man.' [10] This is often overlooked.

In communication theories, it is often assumed that face-to-face communication is on one side and 'media' is on the other. As a result, the two are compared with an attempt to find out which is most effective. Sometimes one media has been used exclusively; but we must look at the whole composite media-problem, including the communication done by the human body in the form of signs and appearance. We must ask questions such as, who is the listener? where is he? and what is he interested in? We also have to ask questions about the influence of the media on the message, and if the medium in fact does become the message, as McLuhan says. How does all the research data collected so far fit together into a meaningful theory that shows the influence of a certain channel, and the inter-relationship in general of all channels?

The Christian Communicator

Christ was the master communicator, and He spoke in terms people understood. He also spoke about matters that concerned His listeners. If we, like Christ, are to succeed in communicating the Gospel, we must learn to speak to the interest of people and to meet their needs. The task of the Church is to share the glorious good news of Christ so that people may be set free. Thousands of men and women still go into eternity every day without knowing Christ and His salvation. Maybe there is a 'lack of communication' and a lack of understanding communications principles. If so, we must correct it. Remember, though, that the use of media in itself is not enough. Without love and dependance on the Holy Spirit to give life to men and women, our tools become 'noisy gongs' and 'clanging cymbals.'

The need for Christian communicators to engage in research will be dealt with and explained in the following chapter. It is not enough for the communicator to understand the message, but also to understand the media and its use. Understanding man, the one who listens to our message, is important. We need to understand him and his attitude to the Gospel and to Christian affairs in general.

The Christian Communication Process

When a man comes to Christ, it is at a certain point in a process that has started maybe months or years earlier. This process should continue for the rest of his life, as he becomes involved in spiritual growth and outreach. The Bible makes it clear that its truth is communicated to man in stages, not all at once. Paul talks about sowing, watering and reaping.[11] A man rarely accepts Christ without having had a series of exposures to the Gospel. It is not the result of a single 15-minute radio broadcast or a single tract. A man must first grasp the basic truths of the Gospel. That often takes a long time, but the importance of understanding is verified by both experience and the Bible message. Most Christian workers will probably admit that it is a process and that the situation demands time. However, if we look closely at much of the so-called evangelism, and specially the use of media, vital parts seem to be missing. Most evangelism seems centered around a relatively small part of the process—the actual conversion. The present need of evangelism, or missions, is not for new one-time approaches, but for a coordinated process that combines media and approaches over a period of time.

Like any other persuasive communication, the amount of time needed for the Christian communications process depends on several factors, such as location, environment, and media. Certain types of commercial persuasion take place over a relatively short time, but if the purpose of a persuasive communicator is political or ideological influence through subtle use of media, the process will of course be much longer.[12]

Communication Models

In order to judge the effectiveness of the various media channels, we have to look at the individual steps involved in a communication, and see them within the framework of the whole. No model is without drawbacks. But, at the same time, a model helps us to visualize the process and purpose of communication and to integrate the various parts of it. Communication has taken place when a message concept has been perceived by the recipient as it was intended by the sender, and has brought about the proper response.

The model shown on figure 6 can serve as a general model explaining the communication process.

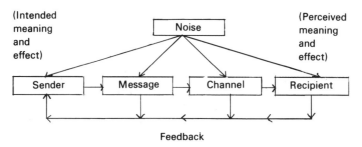

Figure 6
General Communication Model

Effectiveness Influenced by Media Selection

This whole communication process is greatly influenced by a host of different variables which will be briefly discussed later in this chapter. The perceived meaning and effect can deviate substantially from the intended meaning and effect, so at this point it is necessary to identify where the media can and probably will influence the effectiveness of the communication. These areas are:

1. Encoding the message for the media, that is, shaping the message to fit the media.
2. Uniting the message with the media in the actual transmission.
3. Decoding the message from the media by the recipient.

35

This process is seen on figure 7, which is slightly changed from the one above.

Figure 7
Points of Media Influence

Encoding the Message for the Media

Encoding the message for the media refers to the process needed to change or shape a concept into a message or program that can be transmitted by the selected media channel. If the media is radio, the message must be verbalized; if it is television, the message must be visualized. If the media is music-radio, the length of a message must be short—from several seconds up to one minute. For television many messages must be delivered in 30-second or one-minute capsules. A message that is to be transmitted by media which, by the cultural and social structures, have been given an entertainment function, must meet the criteria for drama or some kind of enjoyment.

Uniting the Message with the Media

During the actual 'communication time' the message is united with the media; any limitations of the media will also govern the effectiveness of the message. If the 'media' of inter-personal communication is used, then a person's body may add dimensions to the message—or cause it to be rejected. A printed message can be read only by literates. Any type of electronic media requires a radio, cassette-player, or a television set. The message brought into the living room by television will be presented on a small two-dimensional screen, often in black and white only. The credibility generally ascribed to a certain media by society will also influence the acceptability and credibility of any message presented by it. Programs surrounding the message will influence the selection of audience to be exposed to the message.

Decoding the Message from the Media

If all variables are accounted for, the recipient will receive the message; but this still does not guarantee that he will perceive it the same way as was intended. Again, media influence is important. Is the message presented during a stationbreak while the viewer's attention might be on other matters? Is it presented in a magazine that is outside his general interest range? Does the viewer/listener/reader regard a specific media as a propaganda tool and so completely distrust it? Is his educational background so limited that he cannot grasp what is said? Many other points could be raised, but these are all variables that influence the 'decoding' of a message. They must be accounted for in general strategy and planning, as well as in programming.

The Filtering Process

During the decoding, or reception, process, each message that reaches a person must first pass through a 'filter,' a conscious and unconscious selectivity that a person engages as the message reaches him. It consists of exposure, attention, comprehension, and retention.[13] This selective filter is active for all kinds of communications, but the degree of use may vary on the media, program content and format, as well as on stored information and personality.

In order to get our total Christian message through this filter, a multimedia approach is most effective. If, however, the same media is used for the total process, or the total message covering the various segments, then program type must be changed for the various stages in order to break through the filter and fulfill our total objectives. On figure 9 an attempt is made to show this whole process, but the selection of four different individual messages and media channels to communicate the total message is arbitrarily chosen. There may be many more needed. The four (or more) channels may be different media, or they may conceivably be the same media programmed differently.

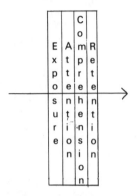

Figure 8
Selective Filtering Process

COMMUNICATION MEDIA

Most studies done on the effectiveness of various media channels seem to have overlooked the fact that the channels are different, and are created for various types and purposes of communication. They seem to be based on the assumption that all media channels are supposed to be able to do the same thing. The effectiveness of the media channel is judged accordingly, that is, how effectively it performs that specific task.

The study of the effects of communicaton has seen a tremendous change during its short history. In the beginning, the effectiveness was taken for granted; but during the last 30 years or more many new theories have been developed. It is evident from published research data that many studies have been grossly biased by the group doing the research. Very little research has been done among Christian organizations, and only recently have some organizations seriously begun researching media effectiveness.

"Who says what, in which channel, to whom, with what effect?" This question by Lasswell leads us to the main question. It is not enough to ask, "Which media channel

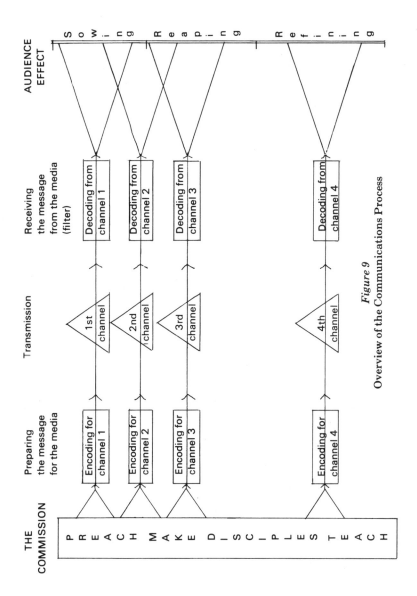

Figure 9
Overview of the Communications Process

39

is most effective?'' because we then have to ask, "Effective to do what?'' Media does not operate in a vacuum, but within a culture. As that culture varies from place to place, from country to country, from home to home, and from individual to individual, so the effectiveness of individual media channels varies accordingly.

Culture defines the language of the media, and the social structure defines the situation.[14] In one culture television is used mainly for entertainment, totally financed by commercial enterprises. In another, it is used primarily as a news and educational source; and in a third culture, television is utilized mainly for propaganda.[15] All of these variables influence people's attitudes toward a particular media channel, and in turn influence its effectiveness in persuasive communication.

The language of media can also be described in terms of its effectiveness to convey certain messages. Each media is uniquely fitted to do a certain range of tasks, and we must analyze this when trying to compare them. For example, music-radio is less effective in conveying straightforward information than the printed word, but news-radio may be equal. However, motion-picture is sound plus moving pictures, and as such adds new dimensions.

Marshall McLuhan explains the various media in terms of 'hot' or 'cold,'[16] but this also has its difficulties. Whether a medium is hot or cold seems to depend more on how that medium is programmed rather than on the medium as such, so different media channels can be used as either 'hot' or 'cold.' When working within only one culture, we can use McLuhan's definition in a limited way; however, it becomes difficult when we enter other cultures that use the media differently. Each medium is effective to do certain specific things. One goal may be reached equally effectively in two different societies by two different channels; but it is not probable that one goal will be reached in society by two different channels.

Audiences differ in their acceptance of the message from various channels. Demographic differences such as age, sex, income, and education also influence exposure and acceptance. There are many questions that can be asked about the 'message-recipient.' Is he a viewer, a listener, or a reader? Does he seek reality, fun, and excitement? Is he a perfectionist, or the self-improvement type?

Does he come to the media as an escapist, or is he coming for specific interest purposes? All of these needs are met by the various mass media, depending on their characteristics and cultural variables.

On the following few pages a brief analysis is made of some of the media we use in Christian outreach. The purpose is to point out differences that we need to understand if we are to plan an effective strategy.

Radio

The most widely used mass media in Christian work is radio. Its advantages are many, but it has its limitations, too. In the hands of those with knowledge, means, and courage, radio is a powerful and effective tool. Although Christian radio has had plenty of spokesmen, there have also been many critics. Some of the major difficulties have been vaguely defined goals and purposes, and the relative lack of training of those who have used it.

Radio is a fantastically flexible tool with many uses. After the onslaught of TV, many expressed the doom of radio, but radio has come back strongly and established itself as a medium in its own right with its own peculiarities. Radio can do certain things no other media can. For example, as long as people have a receiver, radio can reach them everywhere—even while they are engaged in doing something else. There is no screen to watch, no reading to do, no records to turn, and no other people to rely on.

It was the transistor that changed the possibilities for radio, and has made it a medium that, far more than any other, easily accepts flexible adjustments in the face of changing conditions in social and cultural systems. Radio has become a personal media, a one-to-one media.

Radio has many faces. There are News Radio, Music Radio, Talk Radio, Rock Radio, Religious Radio, etc. One country uses radio one way and another country adds new uses. Radio listening is also increasing. In the United States the average number of radio sets per home is now 5.3.[17] Cars have radio. Busses that travel rural roads in Thailand have radio. The farmer riding his buffalo has a radio. The transistor radio is everywhere.

Technically we can reach most people through radio,

but the main question is, "how?" The reason for the lack of apparent results in many places seems to be related to the type of programming done. It was earlier explained that each person engages a filter of selectivity which governs exposure, attention, comprehension and retention.[18] Exposure is greatly influenced by station selection. Program format will influence attention, and program content will largely govern comprehension and retention. Generally speaking, Christian radio stations are not reaching the non-Christian. So, for evangelistic purposes, we either have to use secular stations or change a Christian station's image so the desired audience will tune in. The selection of stations shown on figure 10 seems most effective.

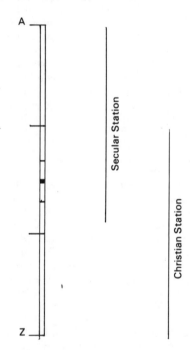

Figure 10
Suggested Station Selection for Christian Programs

Christian radio programming should be carefully analyzed to see if it really is evangelistic and if it is relevant to the intended audience. Programs produced in London, Detroit, or Houston may mean nothing to the Oriental listener, who has a different understanding and spiritual status, a different education and background, and a different religion and cultural environment.

As mentioned before, radio can do many things for us. Here is a list of advantages and possibilities.[19]

1. *Radio can give knowledge and widen horizons.* Expanding people's knowledge and understanding of Christianity can effectively be done on radio.

2. *Radio can focus attention on the teachings of Christ.* By bringing a certain subject to people's attention over the radio that subject becomes a topic of conversation. In some countries Christianity has been a taboo subject for years. After hearing a Christian program on the air, one villager commented, "When the government allows it on radio, it can't be all that bad."

3. *Radio can raise aspirations for change.* If a man listens to another man on the air telling the way God has changed his life, the listener may, by identification with the speaker, aspire to see the same changes in his own life. A positive climate for change may be the result.

4. *Radio can confer status on a weak church.* A ridiculed Christian, or small Christian church in a village or town, will receive recognition and status by the very fact that Christian programs are on local radio stations. If the program carries the testimony of a prince, or well-known filmstar, recognition will be even higher.

5. *Radio can influence social norms.* The social acceptance or rejection of Christians can be greatly affected by Christian radio broadcasting. News of official government recognition can help greatly, too.

6. *Radio can help form tastes.* The matter of music has been a problem in many churches on the mission field. The translation of Western hymns and use of traditional Western tunes by missionaries and national Christians, has often caused rejection of local, indigenous music, giving the church a foreign face. Radio can help to change such a situation and help form tastes for locally written hymns.

7. *Radio can help to change attitudes.* Though it will

43

be difficult to change strongly held attitudes by radio alone, it can be done over time. By working step by step, the strongly held attitudes may gradually change.

8. *Radio is believed, and in time will give a good understanding of Christian words and concepts.* In countries where radio is primarily used as an information source, it is much more readily believed than in countries where it mainly fulfills an entertainment role. Through daily programming, and using only nationals as speakers, singers, and announcers on Christian programs, a true picture of the Church can be communicated.

9. *Radio gets into closed homes.* In many countries it may be almost impossible for a man with higher education, or a high status in the community, to come to a Christian meeting. Yet, he is usually interested in finding out what the Christians are really teaching. Radio can solve that problem.

10. *Radio can, for the same outlay, reach more people.* The task of bringing the Gospel to all men is so enormous that only through skillful and vigorous use of radio does it seem possible.

Many more points could be raised, but these are enough to indicate the importance of radio in our outreach. At the same time, it should be clear that the major strength of radio is in the sowing stage of our task, and that special programming must be utilized to realize the full potential of radio outreach.

Television

The aspirations among Christian workers to use television are not lacking, but so many problems are in the way that very few have used television so far. Before giving suggestions, let us look briefly at the medium.

Due to its sight, sound, and motion, television has the greatest potential as a communication media. In spite of the relatively high financial outlay, it was immediately utilized in countries around the globe. In the United States television required only a decade to reach saturation point because the social and cultural conditions facilitated its growth in many ways. Society had achieved a level of technology which permitted mass manufacture of receiving equipment at a price within the means of the ordinary citizen. Also, broadcasting patterns were already established and a huge pool of entertainment talent was available from film, stage, and radio. Financial base was copied from radio. Television was a new medium which fitted remarkably well within the personality, social, and cultural systems of the society to which it was presented.

To get a true picture of the possibilities and effectiveness of television, we have to look outside the United States as well. In each country the social, cultural, political, and historical circumstances which surround the broadcasting operations are different. In the United States the television media is primarily an entertainment media. In countries with totalitarian regimes, it becomes a tool of political propaganda and indoctrination. In some countries television is primarily used for educational purposes; in others, for news and cultural programs. These factors influence television's own effectiveness as well as its effectiveness for religious purposes. In the United States many studies have been undertaken which tend to prove that television is ineffective in changing attitudes.[20] The political debates have been cited as examples, in particular the debate between Nixon and Kennedy. But does such serious information fit into the context of an entertainment media such as U.S. television? Did the viewers think of entertainment, education, or politics? Did they look at it as just another quiz show? Similar comments could be given about the seeming failure of anti-smoking commercials on television. If smoking is associated with relaxation and entertainment, can the viewer expect the entertainment media to be serious when they condemn smoking? In other countries where commercial television does not exist, and where it is mainly used for news and educational purposes, the same programs might have had much greater effect.

There are several other points to keep in mind when one is "encoding" a message for television. Television uses both audio and visual signals, so everything has to be coded into these two "languages." In an entertainment context the programs must capitalize on drama and conflict. The television audience is large, so the common denominator governing reception will be narrow. This also influences the selection and presentation of material on television. The high cost of time forces the user to concentrate his message in the shortest possible time segment.

Everything transmitted by the television media will be presented on a two-dimensional screen that has a fixed 3x4 ratio size. In many cases it will be in black and white only. Depth, color, atmosphere, surroundings and many other important aspects might be lost in the process. TV brings the communication directly into the living room of millions of people at one time. This adds tremendously to the effectiveness of the media, but it also adds to its problems—and influences the message. In the living room we have, for example, free flow of all kinds of prejudices—color, religion, social, sexual, national, generational. Television records everything through a lens which might be wide angle or it may be close-up. Only one is used at a time. The selection of lenses can influence the image that television gives to the viewers.

According to McLuhan, television is a 'cool' media that requires a lot of participation by the viewer. Here we have to remember that television is used for entertainment, news, information, education, propaganda, or other specific purposes. The viewer will accept the message according to his understanding of the media channel itself. What state of mind, or mood, is he in when viewing television? The credibility of the media and the sources that generally use television will also affect the way a message is received.

It should be mentioned that due to its high cost, television's reception is limited in many countries; however, taken all together, television is a most powerful, effective media if its limitations and possibilities are fully understood and utilized by its users. The communicator who understands to talk quietly and intimately with the family who kindly invited him into their home will also be most persuasive and effective.

In our Christian outreach, then, the question is, for which part of the total program can we, or should we, use television? It is not only the possibilities it gives for sending out the Gospel, but also the tremendous need for good, positive programs that compels us to seriously consider television programming. During the discussion on what radio can do, several points were mentioned, Most of these are also true for television. There is a tremendous need to produce good, effective, and truly evangelistic programs that reach people where they are. In many countries, the governments are even asking for them! There is also a great need for educational programs. Dedicated, well-trained Christian television producers could make a tremendous impact on a country by producing good, positive educational programs. There may also be many opportunities for news or feature programs that analyze world events in a truly objective way. Another area of need, especially in developing countries, is to provide teachers who are able to train national staffs in television and communications as a whole.

Christian workers in more advanced communities should not forget the possibilities of utilizing Community Antenna Television (CATV) systems. Christian Bible teaching programs or Sunday school could be conducted that way, too.

Video Cassettes

Audio cassettes have had immediate acceptance by Christians. Do video cassettes await a similar acceptance? So far there has been some experimentation, and the video cassettes do, in fact, have the capabilities of becoming a major tool in Christian communications. All that is needed is a video cassette player that plugs into the television set.

Superficially the use of the video cassette may look like ordinary television, but it is a very different tool. An important stage is introduced, in that there is only one audience at a time. It becomes a "personal" media, for the video cassette will be used by a person. For evangelistic use it may be a Christian playing it in his living room for some friends. This will require new types of programming, programs that are tailored not only for the new media but also to specific purposes.

The initial extensive use of video cassette in Christian work will probably be in the area of teaching Christians; here it has tremendous possibilities. Some of the points raised later in this manual concerning programs for the audio cassette can be applied to the video cassette as well.

There is no reason why the video cassette cannot be an important evangelistic tool. In our Western societies we must look for new, effective ways of evangelism. The home or small group approach has great possibilities. For this approach the video cassette will be used by a person basically to reinforce his testimony; however, special programs could also be used to open the discussion and witness. Programs might be built around music, drama, Bible teaching, panels, or testimonies. They could conceivably provide a similar help in developed countries as the audio cassette has given in other countries.

Films

Like the video cassette, the use of motion pictures distinguishes itself from the use of television and radio by the fact that only one audience is viewing the film at a given time, and the user of the "tool" will be there in person. This greatly limits the audience size but, on the other hand, has the advantage of immediate feedback and follow-up.

Potentially, there are few media more persuasive than film. As the viewer sits in a darkened theater or room, all the action is brought to him. Limited effort is needed, for all the action is on the screen. Others have shot the film, edited it, etc., so the viewer is spared all the difficult work. In minutes he can travel thousands of miles and span centuries of history.

In many developing countries, films are used in commercial enterprises and in educational projects. This has proven to be most effective as a means of drawing people together and then presenting the message in the context of the film.

The film industry has been slow in redefining its role after the coming of television, but lately there have been new signs of change. The possibilities that film has to communicate may be more fully explored in the years ahead.

The latest developments for film is to record them onto video cassettes. Though there has been some initial success with such projects, one would expect that a new type of programming will be necessary for video cassettes. Some Christian film producers are also talking about doing the same thing, but they should be cautious and study the differences between film and video cassette closely beforehand.

The great advantage of films in Christian work is the immediate feedback and follow-up. The stage of the communications process where this medium is most effective and needed is the actual reaping stage, i.e., leading people to Christ. Since experience indicates that this is true, in terms of the model, it is from J to N that films are most effective. This does not mean that films cannot be used for other areas as well.

Literature

Literature, the oldest mass media, has been used in all aspects of Christian work. Many people believe that literature is the most effective, far-reaching media, but it, too, has serious limitations.

What are the language skills of the receiver or reader? In the United States less than 6 percent of the population is considered functionally illiterate (i.e., unable to read and write at a high enough level to make use of written materials in their daily lives). But for every individual who cannot read at all, many more cannot read at a level that would make persuasive written communication an effective form. Although such individuals can read, it is hard work for them and written messages are avoided in favor of oral messages. For these individuals—and they may constitute a majority of the adult population of the United States, though not the most influential—spoken messages are the only realistic message form.[21] In many developing countries the situation is much worse than in the United States. Though elementary schooling may be compulsory, the standard may not even reach the functionally literate level. In some countries it may not be realistic to expect to reach even 10% of the population by print.

For those who can read, literature is very important and we cannot do without it. Literature was the medium chosen by God to record His dealings with men. God himself wrote the commandments with His own finger, and today that same message is being reproduced in millions of copies by highly developed printing and photographic equipment.

There does exist a 'climate of learning' between this medium and the individual. The attention must be given to the reading totally, and only one person is reading at a time. Comprehension is helped by the possibility of re-reading. A magazine or book will generally carry high credibility on the subject matter it promotes. Selectivity of exposure is a more difficult problem for the print media. Color, title, expense, language, and distribution system are influential factors.

Literature has been used in evangelistic outreach, but its effectiveness has often been limited because of the ir-revelant text used. Too much has been expected of the reader. During the last decade or so, new unique literature ministries have been developed. The publication of the Living Bible deserves mentioning first among these, and so does the increasing use of national writers. Another ministry that could be mentioned is the British-based *Soon* ministry that keeps its vocabulary to 1000 words.[22]

In more advanced stages of missionary work, such as the technical stage, literature provides us with the bulk of our material. For theological education at all levels, literature has so far been the only realistic media to use.

Supplementary Media

The preceding media have all been media that could, if necessary, be used for all aspects of our ministry. Their individual strengths and weaknesses must be studied first, though, so that the best "media-mix" can be selected. There are a number of other tools also used in Christian work, but they cannot practically be considered on the same line as television, radio, cassettes and literature. One of these supplementary ministries is the telephone ministry which is used to give prerecorded messages to those who call in. It is very effective in radio follow-up for spiritual help, and counselling is available on the phone 24 hours a day.

Another medium used extensively in missionary work is the grammophone record.[23] Some advantages of the records are that they are relatively inexpensive, there is no need for expensive equipment to play them on, no bat-teries to buy, and they are very simple to operate. These advantages have made records valuable evangelistic tools during the past many years. One of the main disadvantages of records is the short time available on each record. Tech-nical developments have produced other tools that supersede records in many ways. Records and record players are usually heavy and bulky, so in weight as well as in sound quality, they are inferior to cassettes. If mistakes are discovered in the program on a record, there is no way of correcting it on the field. Future use of gospel records will most likely be in very primitive areas.

One further supplementary medium that can be used effectively is the billboard and poster. Well-made and well-placed billboards can effectively increase the impact of a radio or television campaign. People are exposed to the billboard as they drive past it. But whether it will attract their attention or not depends on such factors as size, color, and creativity in copy and design. Billboards by themselves will probably not be effective in communicating a message, but research studies have shown that they greatly improve the effect of a radio or television campaign.

Summary

Several other tools or media could be mentioned, but those already discussed are enough to illustrate the situation. In order to sum up the main results of this study, it can be said that radio and TV seems most effective at the sowing stage. Their wide coverage and ability to reach into homes without the need of a person makes them invaluable in outreach. A person present is much more needed at the reaping stage, so the film ministry is an effective tool here. At the same time this limits the use of films in the sowing stage. The audio cassette was discussed in the first chapter of this book and will be treated extensively later; but, as compared to other media, the cassette is basically a teaching tool. Used by a Christian, it is effective primarily in areas where teaching is needed. In some countries or in some segments of the population, literature will be able to reach all stages of the missionary task; but for the vast majority of the world's population, its effectiveness in evangelism is limited. At the teaching stage it is very valuable. Use of the video cassette is still very limited but, as television sets are already present in most homes (in the West) and as more cassette players become available, the video cassette has great possibilities for the areas stretching from the latter part of the sowing stage and on to leadership training. Figure 11 illustrates the general comparative media effectiveness.

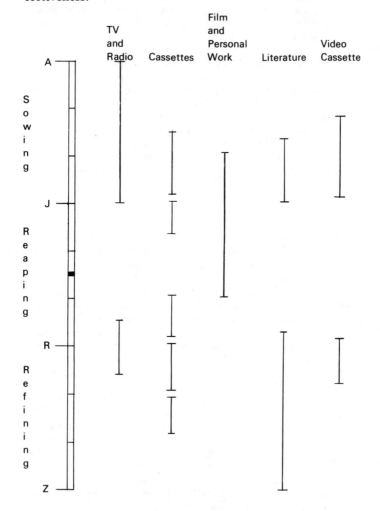

Figure 11
Media Effectiveness (General Model)

52

The media situation will change from country to country for media availability is different, as are the political and social conditions. These factors all influence media effectiveness and use, and they will influence our strategy. In the Scandinavian countries, for example, there is no commercial radio and television available, as broadcasting facilities are operated by the governments, but then these countries have 100% literacy.

CHAPTER 3

Research and Strategy

(Analyzing the Environment of the Cassette Ministry)

In order to fully apply the principles set forth in this manual, and to make use of the model in effective programming and strategy, a certain amount of research will have to be conducted first. Many missionaries and other Christian workers may feel that they already know the answers, or may be tempted to rely on their intuition instead. However, research is necessary. The research designs—and explanations—have been kept as simple as possible, both in language and in structure. Those who are interested in detailed research and statistical analyses should study the suggested books on the subjects.[1] It must be emphasized, though, that the research principles must be followed closely to get valid inferences from the results. While experienced missionaries should be consulted in deciding the research sample(s), their answers should not take the place of research results.

In this planning process there are certain steps that must be followed if we are to arrive at a valuable strategy. The first step is to analyze the environment, that is, a spiritual segmentation of the population, and show the results on the model, then analyze their attitudes and purposes in life. An analysis of the media and their use is also needed. Following that an analysis of the present Christian outreach and of internal resources such as personnel, facilities, and finance should be made. With this background measurable goals can be determined and strategy planned. Finally, the individual programs needed to fulfill the total program can be worked out.

Before we enter into the details of research, there is one point that should be reemphasized—and that is, the overall purpose of the missionary task. This task is to obey the Great Commission given by our Lord; the objectives of all ministries is to build the Church. The commission was given to the Church, so missions—or the task of fulfilling the commission—belongs to the Church. Yet today much Christian mass media work seems to go on outside the Church. But it is the Church, the body of believers, that should be using the media as tools to further their ministry. Those who are engaged in mass-communications should integrate the work with the general outreach of the Church. The ineffectiveness of much work may have its roots in the ignorance of this basic concept. The biblical concept of the "Body" is one that works together in unity, not in disintegration. Therefore, it is valuable for us during the research and planning stage to keep in mind that the fundamental purpose is to see local churches growing and multiplying. Whether we like it or not, the success of our ministry—and, in particular, mass media ministries—will, to a large extent, depend on the local church. It is, therefore, important that the overall strategy be made in consultation with the local churches.

RESEARCH NEEDED FOR THE SPIRITUAL SEGMENTATION OF THE POPULATION

The first step is the actual segmentation of the population on the model. As the differences are so many between the Christians and the non-Christians, we will have to research the "sowing" and the "refining" stages separately. They are in many ways equally important, but the "sowing" stage is treated first; that is, how do you draw the curve between points A and J on the model?

Spiritual Segmentation of the
Non-Christian Population

For the segmentation we could conceivably use either the cognitive or the affective variables. The "congnitive" is understanding the Gospel, and the "affective" is the emotions, or attitude, toward it. This latter point is most important when working on the programming for the various stages, so it will be taken up again at a later point. But for the segmentation, we will use the cognitive variable.

What is the difference between the man who is indicated at point A and the man who is at point J on the model? There is no easy answer. The man at point A knows nothing, but what does point J indicate? He is the man who Jesus said "understands and receives" and is the "good soil" that later produced much fruit.[2] He is at the crucial point (seen from a cognitive point of view), ready for harvest. The question could be raised, what is the minimum a man must understand to represent the "good soil"? Based on experience, research, and interviews with missionaries and national leaders, it has been found that an understanding of the following three general concepts seems to be needed in each case,

1. The concept of God.
2. The concept of man.
3. The concept of salvation.

In researching the effectiveness of Western-produced evangelistic material in Eastern cultures, the same points came up clearly. Some societies teach some of the concepts in school or through their culture. A man in the West will have a certain understanding of the Christian concept of God, while a rural person in South East Asia may have no knowledge of a personal God.

The order of the three general concepts is not emphasized and, in the tabulation of the survey results, they are mixed together. There are some indications that in most cultures the understanding comes in the stated order, but the underlying principle is universally applicable.

We cannot say that every person must necessarily understand all of this before accepting Christ as his Savior. But, if not, a good follow-up plan where these concepts are immediately and thoroughly taught must be used.

Experiences from many places indicate that we will otherwise have a repetition of what Christ was pointing out in the parable of the Sower: The seed never produced fruit.

A number of questions or points that cover these general concepts then needs to be constructed. How these questions are phrased and how the research design is made depends to a large extent on the country, culture, and local situation. The most important point is not to be able to draw an accurate curve on the segmentation model, but to be able to understand where the population is so that effective communication can be made. The main thing is to get an accurate picture of what the population understands about the Christian Gospel.

The Sample

Sampling is the process of selecting interviewees. A probability sample is not suggested due to the need for time, cost, skill, and experience in research. On the other hand, we cannot use certain "convenience samples" that might be available in the form of mailing lists based on radio response, or the families of Christians. Such samples would almost certainly be so biased that a true picture would not be obtained.

Certain demographic characteristics will separate the population into groups, so it will probably be necessary to make sure that different groups are included in the sample. This will call for some kind of stratified sample.[3] Advice from experienced workers can help in deciding which groups must be treated separately. There may be one major ethnic or cultural group in the country covering 80% of the population, another group 10%, and so on. The minor group might, on the other hand, be very important. The population will also be made up of educated young people, illiterate farmers, government officials, children, and old people. Enough groups must be included to give a truly representative sample, yet too many groups will make it cumbersome and will require too large a sample to be valid. The results should be both tabulated separately by strata and also in one complete tabulation for the segmentation. Individual strata results will help in the programming as well as in strategy planning.

For the purpose of this manual, let us suppose that

a given country has a population of 10 million. One important minority ethnic group counts for 1 million. Most people are farmers and live in villages. Small towns are growing. A big gulf exists between the educated young and their relatives. We will then decide on a stratified sample to include 4 groups.

1. The farming population.
2. Children.
3. Young people in towns.
4. An ethnic minority.

A sample of 1200 with 300 from each group would be ideal, but for present purposes a total sample of 400 can suffice if random selection is used. If the samples are not chosen by random we cannot use statistical procedures to obtain results. The random selection of respondents might be carried out as follows:[4]

Group 1. Split the 100 respondents equally between 5 or more villages. Each village should have equal chance of being selected. Then obtain the number of households in the village. If the number is 80, then each fourth house should be used. A number between 1 and 4 can be drawn to decide on the first house and then proceed from there to every fourth house. The respondents should preferably be equally divided among men and women, with various age groups represented.

Group 2. The children might be obtained in a similar way as described above. Otherwise, randomly select 5 schools. Then randomly select the class for each school. (The selection could be forced in such a way that only one class from a certain grade can be used.) Then obtain permission and cooperation from the teacher to have the students fill out the questionnaire.

Group 3. It will be more difficult to obtain an adequate sample among young people in towns. Care should be taken to make it representative. Sampling may be conducted in schools, colleges, places of work, or in parks.

Group 4. The sampling of the ethnic group will all depend on the group and its peculiarities. Remember that each person should have an equal chance of being selected, in order for the research to have representative value.

The actual field approach will have to vary from place to place. Anthropologists have found that unstructured in-depth interviewing has been most effective in rural areas. If well designed, a direct, structured interview might be used in some cultures. In Thailand, H. P. Philips found that a certain sentence completion technique was the most reliable in getting the right or true results.[5] Some combination of techniques might be called for. It might, in some cases, be helpful to use an in-depth type of interview, partly disguising the questions. A tape recorder would be most useful in such a situation. For children in school, a self-administered questionnaire would be used. (In attitude research, direct questioning would not be valid.)

The Questionnaire

Based on the three basic concepts mentioned earlier (the concept of God, man, and salvation), a list of questions must be worked out.

1. Who is God?
2. Where is God?
3. Who is Jesus Christ?
4. How did this world begin?
5. Can you see God?
6. Does God have power over evil spirits?
7. Does God love you?
8. Can God hear you and answer you?
9. What is the difference between God and man?
10. What is sin?
11. Have all men sinned?
12. What is salvation?
13. Does Jesus have anything to do with salvation?
14. How can a man be saved?
15. Does Jesus love everybody?
16. What is the Bible?
17. Describe a Christian.
18. Do you personally have to be concerned about God, sin, and salvation?

Figure 12
Topics for questions to be used for spiritual segmentation of
non-Christian population
(A to J)

In order to tabulate the results, the list of questions must be used in each interview, with a response received to each question. After research and testing with missionaries and national workers from different countries, a list of basic questions has been worked out. The translation of these questions and adaption to each situation will be left to the researcher concerned. The questions cover areas needed for segmentation.

It should be emphasized that the questions in figure 12 do not appear as they should appear on the questionnaire itself. They are the topics that must be dealt with in the individual questions. Language and culture will determine how the actual questions should be worded, and the questionnaire should be thoroughly tested within the culture and language before actual use.

Tabulation of Results

Different methods might be used but here are two suggestions.

Method 1. Tabulate the results simply as Right=1 and Wrong=0. There are 10 steps on the model between A and J, but since A is 0, the highest obtainable number of points should be 9. There are 18 questions used, so simply divide the total by 2, and the respondents place on the model is decided.

Method 2. Record the results on a 0-5 continuum with 0 as complete wrong answer and 5 as complete right answer. This can be much more accurate than Method 1 if the responses are graded exactly alike. When several interviewers are used, they could be asked to record the answer in a sentence. An editor can then go through all answers and grade them. The accumulated points would then be divided by 10 to record the results on the model. "A" is again the person with no right answer.

In our sample of 400, there were 4 distinct groups represented equally. The results might then look as indicated on figure 13.

The sample of 400 was drawn from a population of 10 million. If the sample groups had given similar results, then each number should be multiplied by 25,000, to give the estimates of the whole population. In our stratified sample the 4 different groups gave quite different results, so it is necessary to treat them separately. It might be necessary to treat each group separately on separate models; but for an overall segmentation, the individual results should be multiplied by proportion before recording them on the model.

Points	Group 1	Group 2	Group 3	Group 4	Total
0	20	8	2	0	30
1	53	15	10	2	80
2	20	60	25	5	110
3	5	10	40	10	65
4	2	4	10	24	40
5		2	3	25	30
6		1	3	16	20
7			2	8	10
8			3	7	10
9			2	3	9
	(100)	(100)	(100)	(100)	(400)

Figure 13
Results of Survey

Points	Sample 1	Sample 2	Sample 3	Sample 4	Total
0	1,000,000	160,000	40,000		1,200,000
1	2,650,000	300,000	100,000	20,000	3,070,000
2	1,000,000	1,200,000	500,000	50,000	2,750,000
3	250,000	200,000	800,000	100,000	1,350,000
4	100,000	80,000	200,000	240,000	620,000
5		40,000	60,000	250,000	350,000
6		20,000	60,000	160,000	240,000
7			40,000	80,000	120,000
8			60,000	70,000	130,000
9			40,000	30,000	70,000
	(5,000,000)	(2,000,000)	(2,000,000)	(1,000,000)	10,000,000

Figure 14
Survey Results Multiplied by Proportion

Sample 1: 100 was drawn from a population of 5 million.
Sample 2: 100 was drawn from a population of 2 million.
Sample 3: 100 was drawn from a population of 2 million.

Sample 4: 100 was drawn from a population of 1 million.

Results from sample 1 should be multiplied by 50,000, sample 2 and 3 by 20,000, and sample 4 by 10,000 to give true estimates. The already multiplied points are seen on figure 14.

The numbers in the "total" column above are the numbers that must be put on the models shown on figure 15.

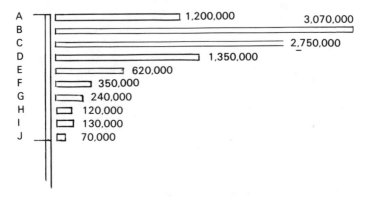

Figure 15
Segmentation Results for the Non-Christian Population

If no consideration had been given to the sampling proportions when recording the results on the model, the curve would have been quite different and inaccurate. In this example an ethnic minority group caused almost all the "high" points, yet their total number is small in comparison to the total population.

Having segmented the non-Christian population on the model, the next step will be to deal with the "refining" stage, that is, the segmentation of the Christians. Further research of the non-Christian population, and programming to the various segments, will be discussed later.

The Christian Segment

The main interest of this section of the Manual is to provide the basis for our programming, regardless of the media used. Segmentation of the non-Christian population had to be based on understanding, but their attitudes will to a large extent influence the type of programming needed to reach them.

Theoretically, we should be able to segment the Christians into groups by a similar method as used with non-Christians—that is, by a cognitive survey based on their understanding of the Bible and its implications for their personal involvement in Christian outreach. We should expect that as understanding of the Bible message increases, so the willingness to be involved would increase, but this assumption is not possible in most instances. Research of understanding will aid us in programming for Christians, but such research should be carried out within each of the following suggested groupings. Programming for Christians, at least as far as cassettes are concerned, will usually depend on their position in the church: "Average" Christians, lay leaders, or fully trained and mature leaders. The research needed for the segmentation of the "refining" stage should, therefore, be done with only a few individuals, namely church secretaries, leaders, Bible teachers, and also from listings in church files or libraries. By adding membership estimates from denominations existing in the country, or area of concern, an approximate number of Christians can be found quite easily. It should also be quite easy to find out how many fully trained leaders or pastors there are. (In the section on cassette programming, some of these points will be dealt with in further detail.)

It will be more difficult to estimate the number of lay leaders, but by close consultation with church leaders and missionaries, and by personal observation, a fairly accurate figure can be arrived at without too much research. The difficulty will be to determine who is a lay leader, as definitions may vary.

In order to clarify this explanation, and to show how the results are recorded on the model, let us say that this research gave the following results:

500,000 Christians in all
20,000 lay leaders
1,000 fully trained leaders

Again it should be emphasized that the most important point is not to be able to position the population exactly on the model, but to visualize the position of the church, so that an effective strategy can be planned and programs produced that reach people where they are. The results should be recorded on the model together with the earlier results, using the same scale of measurement. This will conclude the basic segmentation. The results are shown on figure 16.

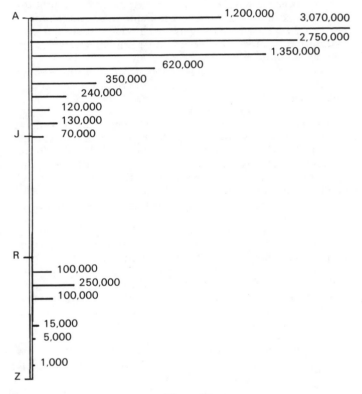

Figure 16
Basic Segmentation Results

RESEARCH OF ATTITUDES

The preceding research, done for initial segmentation, should have given extensive information on which to base our programming, but we should still attempt to obtain as much information as possible about the people concerned. The main areas of interest would be their attitude to the Gospel and to Christian concepts in general, and cultural, social, and political implications of the Gospel. Many of the answers may be partially known by the missionaries and Christian workers, but it would be profitable to do further research and compile the results. In the light of such research, a proper analysis of the present outreach can be conducted and future strategy planned. It should be kept in mind that our major concern in this book is the use of multi media—as compared to inter-personal-communication—so there may not be immediate feedback to show how well we are succeeding in our communication. Therefore, it is mandatory to "know" the audience.

What are the attitudes of the non-Christian to the Gospel and Christians in general? Do they, for example, believe that Christianity is for the white foreigner only, and that to be true nationals they have to follow the national religion? Do they believe that all white people are Christians, and do they judge Christianity by the behavior of all whites —including the personnel at the military base in the vicinity? Such attitudes must be taken into account when we talk strategy and programming. The data may indicate that a person understands a lot, but he may still be hostile to the Gospel.

The cultural and social structures of a country greatly influence the success of introducing church principles. What kind of social groupings do exist and how will these be changed by the introduction of the concept of the Church? How is family life understood? Are the family relations as strong as they were for the Hebrews, or are they weak and unimportant? Does society operate on a status-rank system, making the western way of church life and leadership almost impossible? What kind of behavior is acceptable in inter-personal situations? Do such contacts have to be conducted in a pleasant atmosphere where all possible attempts are made to keep any of the parties from being embarrassed? The answers to such questions may have tremendous implications for the missionary, not only in his daily work and life, but also when he is deciding which communication tools he is going to use in his ministry.

But research is not only conducting surveys. Much information can be gained from secondary sources. Anthropologists have published books or dissertations on some cultural patterns. Books by local authors will also be available and should be studied. Much valuable information can also be obtained by direct observation.

The research needed at this stage may be faced with some serious difficulties and obstacles. Though some approaches are suggested, it should be realized that in many local situations they may have to be adapted extensively in order to be usable. The general topics and concepts should be usable in all situations, but the way in which the information is obtained may vary from culture to culture. The best way to proceed would be to obtain the information at the same time as the initial cognitive information is gathered, using the same sample. (For further information on the Christian population, it might be a good idea to give the same questions to a sample of Christians as well.) For the sake of clarity the following survey is treated as two different surveys, one on attitudes to the Gospel and one on general attitudes and values. The two can follow each other on one questionnaire form.

General Attitudes to the Gospel
and to Christian Concepts

Sampling, discussed earlier, is assumed to have been done in such a way that the following research can be based on it. Our main concern in this part of the study is to obtain delicate information concerning the person's feelings and attitudes which strongly influence a person's willingness to listen or not to listen to the Gospel. His attitudes will influence how or if he perceives the message, or if he will completely disregard it through selective attention and perception. This information can give clues as to which subjects to emphasize in the programs and general outreach.

The method used to learn about a person's attitude is the semantic differential scales. This type of measurement gives insight into the way people understand or view the concepts in question. Then a close analysis of the obtained results must be conducted and serious effort made to find the real causes for the attitudes. The procedure is to have people judge a particular concept on a set of semantic scales, which consist of a number of paired words. These scales are defined by verbal opposites and with a mid-point of neutrality. The concepts we want to test may vary, but the following are suggested,

| Religion | Christianity | Christ |
| God | The Church | Missions |

As an example we will test (or research) the attitudes to the word "Christians." How does a person view a Christian? The paired words used are opposites like 'good' and 'bad.' On the semantic differential scale it looks like this,

Extremely-Quite-Somewhat-Neither-Somewhat-Quite-Extremely

GOOD __ __ __ __ __ __ __ BAD

If a Christian is viewed as extremely good, then check the first space. If he is thought to be neither good nor bad, then check the middle space. In other words, check the space that best describes your opinion of a Christian. Figure 17 shows the suggested questionnaire.

For testing the word 'Christ' some of the pairs may be deleted (eg. 3 and 10), but other pairs could be added like, close-far, sacrificial-non-sacrificial, active-passive, necessary-unnecessary.

A research done in Thailand gave the interesting results of a very positive attitude towards Christ, but a negative attitude towards Christians. The reason seemed to be the close proximity of a foreign military base filled with "Christians" (white soldiers) bringing bad morals.

Tabulation of the results of your research can be done in the same way as suggested with the next part of the research, as indicated on figure 19.

General Attitudes and View of Life

To gain the interest of the listeners and be able to meet their felt needs, one must understand their life-style, view of life, and values. Anyone of these areas might be studied in detail, and several probably have been studied by anthropologists. For our purpose the 5-point continuum on figure

Please check the space on each line that best describe your opinion of a Christian.

	Extremely	Quite	Somewhat	Neither	Somewhat	Quite	Extremely	
Respected	—	—	—	—	—	—	—	Disdain
Intelligent	—	—	—	—	—	—	—	Unintelligent
Educated	—	—	—	—	—	—	—	Illiterate
Tolerant	—	—	—	—	—	—	—	Intolerant
Helpful	—	—	—	—	—	—	—	Harmful
Good	—	—	—	—	—	—	—	Bad
Strong	—	—	—	—	—	—	—	Weak
National	—	—	—	—	—	—	—	Foreign
Relevant	—	—	—	—	—	—	—	Irrelevant
Follower	—	—	—	—	—	—	—	Leader
Productive	—	—	—	—	—	—	—	Unproductive
Real (true)	—	—	—	—	—	—	—	Hypocritical
Warm	—	—	—	—	—	—	—	Cold
Wise	—	—	—	—	—	—	—	Fool
Important	—	—	—	—	—	—	—	Unimportant

Figure 17
Semantic Differential Scale for Attitude Research

18 can be used to indicate a person's view of how important a value or concept is considered to be. The continuum should range from very important to very unimportant as seen in the following example.

Education is	very important	imp.	some imp.	un- imp.	very un-imp.
	—	—	—	—	—

Indicate the space that best resembles your viewpoint for each of the questions on the questionnaire.

When tabulating the results it might be helpful to count how many checks there are in each space and then write that figure in on a blank survey form. (See the example on figure 19.) The best indicator would be to find the median and indicate its position on the form. The median is the "middle score," so in our sample of 400 it is response No. 200 from one side of the continuum. If there were 50 responses in the first space, 170 in the second, 100 in the third, 50 in the fourth and 30 in the last space, the median would be in the second space. Figure 19 gives a hypothetical example of such a tabulation.

In order to have a happy and satisfying life . . .

	very imp.	imp.	some imp.	un- imp.	very un-imp.
1. A good job is	____	____	____	____	____
2. High income is	____	____	____	____	____
3. Happy family life is	____	____	____	____	____
4. Many children are	____	____	____	____	____
5. Religion is	____	____	____	____	____
6. Education is	____	____	____	____	____
7. Pleasure is	____	____	____	____	____
8. A good reputation is	____	____	____	____	____
9. To be respected is	____	____	____	____	____
10. To have peace is	____	____	____	____	____
11. To go to church is	____	____	____	____	____
12. To have friends is	____	____	____	____	____
13. To have a powerful position is	____	____	____	____	____
14. To be honest is	____	____	____	____	____

Figure 18
Research of View of Life

Demographic Characteristics

It will be necessary to obtain demographic information on the questionnaire—age, sex, occupation, etc., of the individual respondents. Cross-tabulation of some results by demographic characteristics may indicate differences between age groups. Such information may also explain the distribution of the obtained data.

In order to have a happy and satisfying life. . .

	very imp.	imp.	some imp.	un-imp.	very un-imp.
1. A good job is	70	140	160	0	0
2. High Income is	290	90	20	0	0
3. Happy family life is	10	100	180	90	20
4. Many children are	20	75	100	125	80
5. Religion is	50	175	100	70	5
6. Education is	150	150	80	20	0
7. Pleasure is	250	125	25	0	0
8. A good reputation is	325	65	10	0	0
9. To be respected is	290	100	150	50	10
10. To have peace is	90	100	150	50	10
11. To go to church is	0	60	100	160	80
12. To have friends is	125	200	50	25	0
13. To have a powerful position is	80	125	90	75	30
14. To be honest is	50	100	120	100	30

Figure 19
Tabulated Research Results

MEDIA RESEARCH

There is one further area of general research that is
important if we are to plan an effective use of media—a

study of the country's use of media and channels of communication. In the preceding chapter different media variables were pointed out. At least some of these should be researched. Some of the data can be collected at the same time as the preceding research by using a simple questionnaire where answers only need to be checked off.

The information needed concerns the availability of communications facilities. How many radio and television stations exist? Where are they located? How far do they reach? What type of programming do they use? What kind of Christian program material is acceptable? Do people read? What do they read? Are newspapers widely distributed? What kind of literature do people really like?

Information about the reception possibilities are important factors. Do people have radios? Are these radios shortwave, AM or FM? How many have television receivers? How many watch each set? Are the owners upper class, or do middle and lower classes also own television sets? Are people able to read at such a level that they can enjoy reading?

We would also like to know how information and news are dissimulated in the communities. Is it by a two-step flow whereby opinion leaders first receive the information from the mass media, and then pass it on to the rest of the community?

The situation for each possible media should be analyzed, and we should be alert to every possibility for Christian use of media. Then on the background of the research data collected so far, it should be possible to tell which media would be most effective at the various stages of our task of bringing out the Great Commission in all its fullness. The results given on figure 11 (page 52) will most likely be similar to those in most countries, but each country will also have its own pecularities and possibilities.

ANALYSIS OF PRESENT OUTREACH

The aim of this manual is to show how audio cassettes can be used effectively in Christian outreach and ministry. They will only be effective if used to meet a need in the work or to improve present methods and ministries. It will therefore be necessary to know what is being done and to what effect. With this information and the results of the preceding research, we can proceed to plan the strategy and, in particular, the use of cassettes.

Some of the information needed will not be difficult to obtain, especially if the reader's interest concerns only one area, with only one mission or church. If several mission groups or churches are involved, then some more detailed interviewing may be necessary. Information is needed on the different types of ministries that are being carried out, the number of workers, and the distribution of workers according to the individual ministries. The stated aim of each ministry and the reported results should also be included.

Following next is one of the most important points in the whole planning process: A critical analysis and evaluation of the present ministries. This is no easy task, and it will have to be left up to the individual to decide how much research he is going to do. Intuition will probably not give the full answer. Scientific research could be the most important eye-opener for any mission in this respect. Some mission boards have counted the cost involved and proceeded to ask a professional research group to do the research for them. In some cases the results have been far from encouraging for the groups as they discovered that they were only reaching Christians when they thought the outreach was evangelistic. Another organization discovered that some of their material was misunderstood completely by the target audience. But such information can be a tremendously important factor in changing the ministries and putting them on a course that truly coincides with the objectives. It is beyond the scope of this manual to enter into details of how this research should be conducted.[6]

The suggestion at this point is, therefore, that the reader draws a segmentation model on a blank piece of paper, and then closely evaluates each ministry on the basis of available data. After this analysis, a line should be drawn where this particular ministry reaches and is effective. The preceding material in this manual, including media characteristics, should be kept in mind during this important analysis and evaluation. (See figure 20 as an illustration of how it might look.)

ANALYSIS OF INTERNAL RESOURCES

The last step before finally setting goals and planning strategy is to analyze available resources.

Personnel

As we are evaluating the whole outreach, the listing of personnel should include those presently engaged in various ministries. It is also important to list part-time workers as well as full-time personnel. Further personnel may be available in the form of short-term missionaries or hired professional help for specific purposes.

Facilities

List all facilities available and their particular possibilities. If the analysis concerns one church or mission only, then list the facilities of other missions or denominations that are available. For example, if cassette production is contemplated, high financial outlays may be avoided by the use of a recording studio belonging to another mission.

Finance

Financial resources are needed for all ministries. What are the total financial capabilities? How much of that is already committed and how much could, if necessary, be made available for a cassette ministry? Are there churches or Christian foundations that may be willing to underwrite certain new developments or projects? A realistic appraisal of the financial needs and possibilities is needed for a realistic strategy.

STRATEGY

Defining Goals

The overall goals of the ministry should now be clearly defined, so that individual parts of the ministry can be seen in the right perspective. The goals may be stated in terms of the model used in this manual or in terms of the questionnaries used. If research has been carried

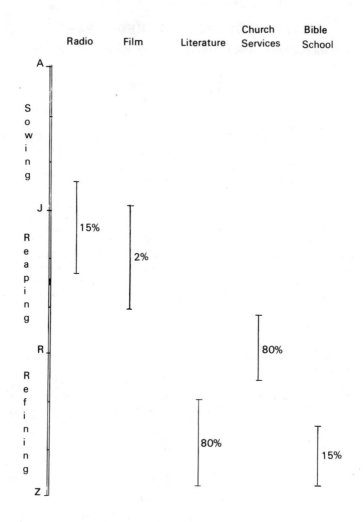

Figure 20

Analysis of Present Outreach (Hypothetical Case)
Percentages indicated are the percentage being reached of that
segment of the population.

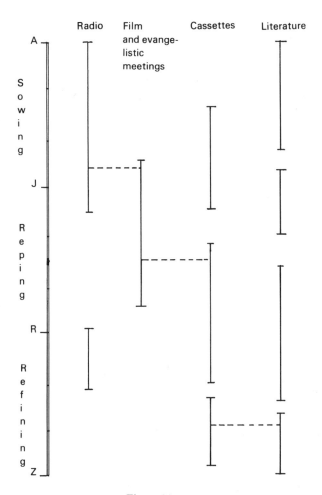

Figure 21
Media Strategy to be used for a Total Program on X Field.
This program is closely integrated with outreach by missions and
local Christians to multiply their ministry. The major thrust and
integration is indicated by dotted line.

out and results are recorded on the segmentation model as shown on figure 16 (page 64), then draw a new model and put in the goals. These are the results that should be obtained if a similar sample is tested with the same questions later on.

The overall goals may also include change of attitude to the Gospel on the part of the non-Christian. If certain negative attitudes were discovered, then the goal might be to change these attitudes. In order to measure if change has occurred, the same questionnaire has to be used.

Determination of the Total Program

Having determined the measurable goals, the next step (on the basis of accumulated research data, analyses and experience) is to determine the strategy or total program needed to fulfill the goals. Goals and purposes of each ministry involved should be clearly defined. A single model will show the integration of all ministries.

The total program should have a major line of thrust from A to Z, but several areas may be duplicated, or reinforced, by different approaches in order to reach all demographic segments. Figure 21 gives a simplified illustration of such a program.

Some of the ministries may be new and may involve training programs for personnel, as well as setting up new facilities. The strategy plan may also state how the responsibilities for the various specific tasks are shared between missions or departments.

The rest of this book deals with how the audio cassette ministries should be handled and used. For information and help concerning other media, other sources of information need to be consulted. The strategy plan will have indicated where the audio cassette is going to be used, but it is assumed here that the decision has been to use it extensively for several segments or parts of the total program. The following chapters will therefore deal with all aspects of how to put a full cassette program into operation.

CHAPTER 4

Organizing the Cassette Project

BASIC PRINCIPLES OF THE CASSETTE PROJECT

Management

Just as a business cannot function efficiently without good management and leadership, neither can a missions-project such as a cassette ministry. Many missionaries and Christian workers have indicated great interest in using cassettes, but they have no time. Therefore, the study of a few, simple principles of management will help such a man, not only do his present job better, but also enter into a cassette ministry that will greatly expand his work.

If a leader is not able to plan and lead, he not only frustrates others, but he is also a poor steward of the responsibilities and gifts God has given him. Under God we are responsible to manage our work, make plans, set goals, and then lead the team in the work needed to achieve these goals.

Managment in Christian work is based on our commitment to God. All our desires are to see His will fulfilled. His primary command to use us is outlined in the Great Commission, and He has given us a special tool, the cassette, to help fulfill His will. To fully utilize this tool and to bring most honor to His Name, a proper management of the project is needed. The hit-or-miss, rule-of-the-thumb approach is inadequate.[1] The one who is going to be in charge of a cassette project will have the responsibilities of setting objectives, training personnel, overseeing productions, and looking after all the other phases of the work. Approaching these problems from a management position will help to solve them in an effective manner.

Operating Policies

A policy is an answer worked out in advance to an anticipated question. It is a rule by which people abide as they work to fulfill their purposes. Such rules should be *in writing*, embodied in a policy manual which is available to everybody directly involved. The purpose of a policy manual is to provide a group of people with consistent answers to recurring questions. Well-conceived policies which are understood and followed by a group enable them to maximize their collaboration toward goals and minimize the amount of energy drained off by friction, uncertainty and confusion; good policies thus maximize the use of energy and time for making progress toward the fulfillment of the set purposes.[2]

The policy statements of a cassette project should include the following six points:
1. Purpose of the Cassette Ministry.
2. Objectives of the Ministry.
3. Quality Standards of the Productions.
4. Scope of Distribution and Cooperation.
5. Financial Policy.
6. Responsibilities for the Project.

1. *Purpose of the cassette ministry.* This may be a broad statement that describes what the desires are. It should include the areas of service we feel called to accomplish—spiritual, educational, social, or medical.

2. *Objectives of the ministry.* This specifies more precisely the goals, and how to reach these goals.

3. *Quality standards of the production.* A cassette project that aims at wide distribution and cooperation, and that expect to have an effective ministry, must aim at professional standards in the areas of production equipment and skills, as well as in program content and presentation.

4. *Scope of distribution and cooperation.* How far are we aiming? Do we expect to utilize only our own church's or mission's personnel and outreach, or do we aim at countrywide distribution? Included in the distribution scope will be the cooperation scope with other denominations in both production and outreach.[3]

5. *Financial policy.* It should be clearly stated how the financial obligations are going to be met—by mission or church, subsidized, nonprofit or profit expectations.[4]

6. *Responsibilities for the project.* Responsibility is here thought of in the sense of sponsorship, and includes not only responsibility for content and finance but also management. In a mission situation where the plans are eventually to turn the project over to nationals, the nationals should be included in the project plans from the very beginning.[5]

If goals and objectives are clearly stated, they can help us to evaluate our work and its progress. They will give a basis for review sessions and meetings, and they can function as the center of the attention of the team or staff. They provide the framework within which to work.

Inter-Mission and Inter-Denominational Cooperation

We all know the situation, though its outward face may change from place to place, from ministry to ministry. There are three recording studios in one town, each run by a different church or mission. No one has adequate studio facilities, yet all have some; none have adequate staff, yet all have some. The result is often mediocre quality in production, with unrelated, duplicated output. There is also the town with several churches, all similar in doctrine and beliefs, yet seemingly competing with each other.

A number of reasons are given for not working together, but a summary is enough for the present. To begin with, there is the lack of knowledge of each other. One mission does not know what facilities the other has; one church knows almost nothing about the other church a little further down the street. There seems to be very little fellowship between groups, and this situation has often led to distrust of each other. Of course there are theological differences, but in many cases they are more imagined than real. Denominational restrictions often hamper cooperation, and there is the desire to have one's own denominational name on everything we print or participate in. Everybody seems to want everything, but few ask if it is needed when *they* have it. Finally, there is the question of supporters. Some missions are under restrictions not to cooperate with certain other groups, even in technical matters.

Even though the above reasons may sometimes seem valid, often prohibiting effective cooperation, yet the situation must change, and it is changing. Cooperation is possible between different denominations, and it can be accomplished without taking away denominational or group distinctions. The advantages of cooperation are many.

1. *No waste of money.* Establishing a cassette project is, like any other communications effort, quite expensive. By utilizing all resources available, top quality, effective production facilities can be established.

2. *Better qualified staff.* All organizations need qualified staff, but they can do far more when they are concentrated in a united effort.

3. *Higher quality.* Effective facilities and qualified staff will produce higher quality. One man alone cannot produce quality in all areas, but by putting experts from various fields together, a high quality is possible.

4. *Smaller staff.* One effective, professional production center will not only do a much better job than several studios, but it will also operate more effectively with a smaller staff.

5. *Works for better understanding and fellowship.* By working together, understanding and trust is built, and little by little the cooperation can be extended to include all areas. This may lead to the situation in which one group specializes in one ministry and another group in another —a coordinated outreach. No valid reason can be given for why we cannot be good stewards and have intermission cooperation in a cassette project, so plan it that way from the very beginning. It is, of course, a necessity that the objectives and scope of operation be defined in such a way that the project will work.

Nationalization Program

The 1970s are different times from the setting of the classic missionary stories that relate how great men opened up countries for the Gospel. Such stories of pioneer missionary work are still very attractive in Christian circles. But the times have changed and the Western missionary is not always welcome. His education may be less than those he is trying to reach, and his Western culture is not only unwanted but not relevant. In fact, the whole concept of Western dominated communications leadership and production is challenged to the very core.

The problem is acute on many fields and in many Third World Christian institutions. If we are to set up an effective cassette project, we had better be realistic and look at the problems. The main problems seem to be that the organizations are built on Western principles and cultural values, they are centered around the missionary and his support, and they concentrate on what the missionary and his group find to be most important. There may be hopes of a national taking over the leadership one day, but the national has not been taught how to do this job within his own cultural background and value system. It would be most difficult for him to take over and lead an organization built on Western principles. Let us be daring and build an organization that puts the missionary and the national as equals, an organization that the national can work in.

Another problem seems to be a lack of acceptance—acceptance of the other as an equal person with value and insight, and who can do an honest job. There are many small ways to reject the other person. A missionary may in some cases do this by just following his own ingrown cultural heritage.[6]

Rejection produces alienation. Rejection of the national by the missionary in matters such as leadership and planning a cassette project as well as other projects, may lead to expressions of nationalism and in turn a rejection of "the outsider." This has sadly enough often led to a rejection of his message as well.

Some of the things we can do to avoid such a situation are:

1. The objectives of the project must be clearly spelled

out. Is it going to be a cassette project of the mission, or is it to be an effective tool for the national church? If it is a tool for the national church, they should help to plan it, though the missionary may be very important in guiding the thinking and planning.

2. It must be a sound organization. We cannot build it around one single person in such a way that if he fails, then the whole thing collapses. The financial situation and principles should be able to operate with changing staffs. Money may be received from abroad, and will be needed, but the discontinuation of such funds should not cause the project to totally collapse. That is why a partnership is important from the very beginning.

3. The national must be a part of the project, and be made to feel so. This following quotation from J. Johnson's book, *The Nine to Five Complex*, is relevant here, though not written to this specific situation.

> To get a man from the empty "I only work here" commentary to the statement of commitment that says "I belong here" is not that big a gap to bridge. It ought to begin with trust, a trust that shows itself on the part of the leader in allowing responsibility or opportunity to create, experiment, and even make mistakes. Trust is cardinal to organizational value. It is a trust born out of a sense of realization that the people sent into the organization are "God sent," regardless of whether the people themselves sense that entirely. It is trust that should be demonstrated by the leader in his willingness to "expose" himself in genuine informal identification with his rank and file, without feeling that it will cancel his sense of "godly authority." A pat on the shoulder, a word of encouragement, even giving a man a job bigger than his capacity, can be the beginning of that emergent "sense of belongingness." [7]

4. The national should receive an adequate salary. Because missionaries get support from home, they are not receiving a "salary" (or so they say!), and they expect the national to go for less pay than he deserves. It is the experience of many that only the organizations which pay a reasonable salary to their employees will succeed. Taking everything into consideration, a national worker is less expensive than a missionary. Missionaries often engage in work they should not do, because their

time is too expensive. Where in a commercial enterprise do you see a college graduate spending his time copying cassettes?

5. Establish effective, long-range training programs. Try to look at the ultimate goals, the time when the nationals will be leading, and begin training him for that day. In the long run, this is the only realistic way to approach the subject, and the sooner in the project such steps are taken, the easier they are.

THE DISTRIBUTION SYSTEM

The Need for a Distribution System

The distribution system covers the span from time of production until the cassette reaches the user. For a church that sells copies of the Sunday service at the door, there is not much to consider. Also, for the missionary who makes his own cassettes and only uses them himself, this section will have little value. On the other hand, for the Christian organization in the U.S., which aims at country-wide sales and the mission organization which serves all missions in the country, the distribution network is of utmost importance. The type of project planned will govern which type of distribution system you will require. The main requirement of a distribution system is to have the cassette available for the user at the time it is needed.

Avenues of Distribution

Most projects will require the use of different avenues for the physical distribution of the cassette. In some projects several avenues may be used, forming an integrated system.

1. *Sales from Christian bookstores.* An organization may center all its distribution on such a plan. The advantages are many if enough Christian bookstores are in existence to facilitate distribution. It would require that a stock be kept at each outlet all the time, which in turn means high financial investment. Some types of cassettes lend themselves more to such a distribution than others.

2. *Mail service.* A distribution centered on mail ser-

vice requires reliable mail service—which is not available in many rural areas of the world. The great advantages of mail service is that it can be operated from a single outlet—the production studio itself, for example—and in that way makes it possible to have a minimum of cassettes in stock.

3. *Church services.* In many cases, the meeting together of the Christians at church is an ideal situation for distributing cassettes to the individual users.

4. *In clinics.* On many mission fields clinics are held at regular intervals in various villages and towns. Such regular meeting places are good for the regular distribution of cassettes.

5. *Missionary journeys or pastoral visits.* If conducted on a regular basis, these may also be an important part of the distribution system.

As mentioned before, most projects will require more than one avenue. The type of distribution—sale, loan, rental, gift—also influences the choice of avenue. A cassette will often travel by mail or from a shop to the buyer who may not be the ultimate user. He, or the church, may in turn lend it to somebody else, or it may be left in a village after a visit there.

The Principle of a Cassette Circle
or the Local Outreach

One of the first missions to establish a separate cassette department was the W.E.C. The department was named "Cassette Circles Worldwide." Some have interpreted the word "circle" to mean that the cassettes should travel from user to user in a circle as indicated on figure 22.

This principle has proved to be too difficult in practice due to several problems. It is difficult to get a user to pass a cassette on at a certain date, so the cassettes may pile up in one place, with the result that some may not get any at all. It has been found that when a special, popular cassette comes along, it is kept much longer, for the user will want to play it for more people. A much more workable system or circle is illustrated on figure 23.

The cassette will be returned to the central library after

84

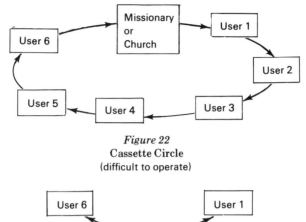

Figure 22
Cassette Circle
(difficult to operate)

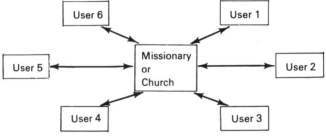

Figure 23
Local Cassette Distribution

use, so that a constant check is available. In order to keep such a system working, the missionary or church must have an adequate file system that tells where the cassettes are at the moment and which ones each user has already had. Many people have started a cassette project or library without such a file system only to find that within a short time the whole project is in a mess. It may be necessary to leave certain cassettes with the user of the cassette player all the time and just change other cassettes around. A Christian may, for example, keep three evangelistic cassettes all the time, but the Christian education cassettes he himself is using are returned after two weeks.

On a national scale the distribution network may look like figure 24 with the exception that more distribution centers may be used and many more local "circles" kept in operation.

Such a distribution system has proved to be effective. The main idea is to establish libraries at strategic places, and distribute materials from there. One mission may operate a big library for their missionaries who in turn operate smaller libraries from various churches.

Another important point learned is that the production studio should not deal directly with the user. One of the main reasons is the difficulty involved in supervision, and the lack of knowledge of the local situation.

However, it should be mentioned here that the distribution of material for a lay leadership training program such as the Cassette Bible School is somewhat different. This will be dealt with later.

Pricing of Cassettes

Pricing cassettes and associated material is not an easy matter, especially among Christians and missionaries. The subject of pricing "services" is rarely discussed openly. But for those responsible for cassette projects, the subject is of utmost importance and must be dealt with in a realistic way. In missionary work, pricing is complicated by the fact that missionaries work "free of charge," supported by their home churches. Some organizations view cassettes as "their" ministry and so expect no financial return. Others have seen good business possibilities in cassettes and have made a good profit. Whatever the policy, producing cassettes costs money, money that has to be paid in one way or another. Even though the objective is not maximum profit, but maximum outreach, an appropriate pricing strategy is an important requirement of a successful cassette project.[8]

Setting Price Policy

Price policy are general principles, rules, or guidelines that should be followed in daily decisions concerning new productions and in agreements with missions and churches about specific outreaches. Some price policies might be:

1. All expenses to be reclaimed in the selling price, or

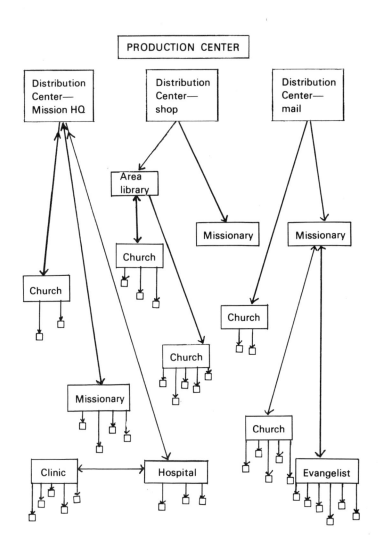

Figure 24
Cassette Distribution Network

2. Only the cost of the cassette to be reclaimed, or
3. 10% profit margin on all sales, or
4. No financial outlays to be reclaimed.

It may be easy to establish the policy, but it is not always easy to follow—or to explain to fellow workers! Commercial prices are usually much higher than Christian cassettes need be, and price policies of other Christian organizations may not fit your situation.

Price Variables

Pricing can be based on various principles, but here the cost factor is used. The five areas that must be taken into account are:

1. The cassette itself
2. The cost of the program material
3. Copy expenses
4. Sales or handling
5. Profit

The pricing is then looked at in the light of the expected total life-cycle of that particular cassette; that is, what is the total number of copies made of that particular cassette?

1. *The cassette.* In a small project where turnover is limited and the stock of cassettes is modest, the pricing is simple. In larger projects, where standard prices are kept, it is more difficult. A shift in brand name may be necessary or the company supplying the cassettes may change the prices—just after you have bought a large stock! When buying in large quantities, a good discount may be obtained; but then there are other expenses such as those involved in the actual purchase (travel), storage in air-conditioned room, and interest on the capital invested in the stock. These expenses may change but, generally speaking, 10% should be added to the basic cost.

Cost of one C60 cassette	$1.80
10% expenses	.18
Resale price	$1.98

(This price may seem high in the United States, but it is an average price in many countries.)

2. *Cost of the program material.* This is the most difficult part to assess exactly, and the most difficult factor

to control if the price of the finished cassette is kept constant. A church just recording a service will not have to figure this cost, unless the pastor or choir gets royalties. Generally, the following areas are included in the expenses,

Script writing
Royalties or wages to speakers and performers
Technical personnel
Master tape
Electricity
Use of production equipment and studio
Testing material

If the recording is of a single voice only, the royalties or wages may be minimal, but music recordings will be quite expensive. Script preparation is minimal for a music tape, but very expensive when producing programmed instruction. The other factors will be more or less the same for each cassette. The use of the equipment includes all hours the equipment is used for both recording and editing master tape. Equipment expenses may be based on an annual 15% depreciation of the equipment: that is, divide total annual operating hours in 15% of equipment cost. For a $15,000 investment this would be a little over $1.00 an hour.

An example is the production of a music tape on the mission field.

Wages and expenses for singers and musician	$40.00
Script (introductions)	2.00
Technical personnel	15.00
Tape	3.00
Electricity (incl. air-conditioning)	3.00
Equipment and studio	15.00
Testing	5.00
Total cost of material	$83.00

If a sale of 100 copies is expected, the material cost should be estimated at $.83. (That means that every time a person copies your material, he owes you $.83!) Obviously, the volume of turnover influences the cost per cassette. In a Cassette Bible School where the script may take three weeks of work, the price of the material may be very high, but other teaching cassettes may be relatively cheap to produce. In the U.S. the turnover may be so large that program material cost will be negligible.

3. *Copy expenses*. High-speed duplicators have reduced this cost. Copy expenses include depreciation of equipment, labor, and checking finished cassettes. The total cost may be only $.25 per cassette.

4. *Sales or handling expenses*. The following factors must be considered.

Publicity
Service
Labelling
Handling and postage
Billing
Retailers profit

For large projects most of these factors will be quite minimal, so maybe $.15 can be allocated to cover all except the retailer's profit. This last factor may not be applicable in some places, but in others it may add 50% to the cost of each cassette. For this present purpose, let us estimate it at $.50, which is only a kind of payment for retailer expenses. This adds up to $.65 for sales and handling.

5. *Profit*. If the organization wants a profit margin, this is added on to the cost price. In our present example, it is left out.

Total Price

By using the above example, the price of 1 C60 cassette (in a volume of 100 expected copies) should be:

The cassette	$1.98
Material	.83
Copying	.25
Sales and handling	.65
Selling price	$3.71

This price gives no profit if 100 copies are sold, and if less than 100 are sold, there is a loss. If a person supplies you with his own cassette, the cost of the cassette can be subtracted, but the person should pay for the cost of the program material.

Special Projects

When another organization asks you to do a special job for them and asks for a price, the following factors should be remembered:

Depreciation of equipment
Upkeep of equipment
Electricity
Staff time

If a certain organization pays for all expenses involved in the production, including making the master tape for the duplicator, checking, labelling, and handling, then you may be able to charge only $.25 for each copy. The same applies if a master tape made to your specifications is supplied.

Cassette Players

There will be several other pieces of equipment or material that you will be asked to supply. By buying cassette players in bulk, you may get a good discount, but it should be remembered that your actual price is higher than the discount price. You will have to include expenses associated with the purchase, cost of keeping stock, investment, service on returned players, and postage. Usually a 10% charge would be right in most places, so if the player is bought for $25, it should be resold at $27.50 just to keep even. No profit will be gained at this price.

Special Policies

It is most important that the actual production price is known, but how the cost is met is secondary. At Voice of Peace a somewhat flexible policy has been kept due to the fact that the studios have served more than a dozen mission agencies, each one having a different financial policy. Some of them resell the cassettes and players; others give them away or lend them out. On the mission field the number of copies for each cassette would be smaller than in the U.S., and so the cost of program material higher. The cassettes are usually also double the price of those in the U.S., but then the high retail profit is often excluded. Expensive productions have been carried by Voice of Peace itself from gifts received directly from abroad. Cost of equipment use is rarely included, for the equipment has been donated and should be servicing all missions.

The Cassette Bible School is very expensive to produce, so the production cost is absorbed by Voice of Peace. Students are only asked to pay for the actual cassettes and copy expenses. Some cooperating missions pay half of that cost and the local church or Christian the other half. Some tribal languages are produced for other groups who pay all expenses involved, except for equipment depreciation. One mission buys the cassettes and players from Voice of Peace at cost price. A Christian worker from the tribe or church the mission works with is asked to pay half the cost of the player, and they receive six cassettes free of charge. After this initial "offer" the mission continues to pay half the price of new cassettes.

The Building of a Distribution Network

To recap and summarize some of the necessary steps, it is important that the distribution system is:

1. Built into the concept and objectives.
2. Built on research, experimentation, and observation.
3. Built on experience in the country.
4. It must include an effective advertising and distribution of news.
5. A good distribution network can only be built on continual good quality, consistency, trust, understanding, and goodwill. This will in turn require continual good public relations to all concerned.

CHAPTER 5

Programming Cassettes
for the
Christian Listener

PURPOSES AND SCOPE OF PROGRAMMING CASSETTES FOR CHRISTIANS

It might seem more logical if the section on programming began with evangelistic programming (or programming to the segment at the upper section of the model), and then worked towards the section on leadership training, but this is not the way cassettes have been accepted for use in Christian outreach. In most places the first and main use of cassettes has been to train the Christians. As indicated on the model (figure 25), this chapter will cover the post-decision stage of the reaping process and the section for the average Christian, which is the first part of the refining phase. It might seem unimportant to program cassettes for Christians since so much other material is available for this audience, but in this instance we are talking about a new tool—a tool that is able to break through many barriers that have obstructed an effective teaching ministry. On many mission fields critical situations have developed due to the lack of teaching. One of these problems is that the church is unable to withstand heresy and sin. Another is the lack of witness by the local Christians.

The cassette project in Thailand began with programming to new Christians. It had been a matter of grave concern to see so many new Christians unable to stand firm in the face of immediate opposition. Some new way had to be found in which obviously needed teaching could be given. The main objectives of the programming were therefore to establish the new Christian in the faith and to help him grow spiritually. It was soon discovered, though, that more established Christians also needed basic training.

For each phase of the cassette programming, there should be clearly stated objectives or goals. The general objectives for a cassette ministry to Christians may be to move a person from being a new-born babe to becoming a mature Christian, or move a person from N towards U on the model. Such a ministry will include both a devotional ministry and a teaching ministry. Each cassette should be produced with specific goals in mind.

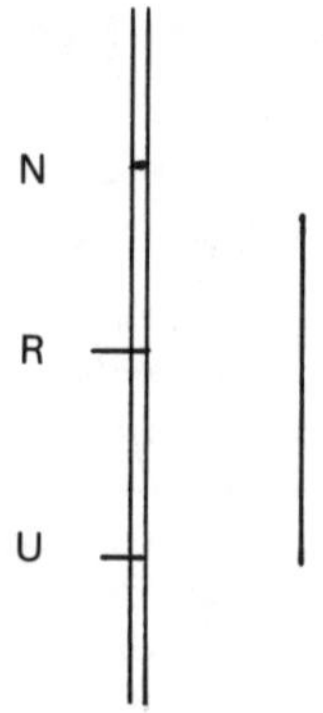

Figure 25
Cassette Programming for Christians

The scope of the cassette programming and ministry should also be defined. The various types of ministry that are needed at each stage can be defined on the model, but the next job is to decide for which of these specific purposes the cassettes are to be used. Strategy was discussed earlier, so now the need is to define these goals and state specific objectives is merely restated. The reasons for being specific are many. We can only do a job, if we know exactly what that job is! Many have discovered that if objectives are specified, the results will greatly improve.

WHY USE CASSETTES IN MINISTRY TO CHRISTIANS?

The best way to answer this question is to compare the cassette with some of the other heavily used media to see if it has any advantages.

The Cassette Versus Literature

In spite of the fact that higher motivation exists in the Christian audience than in the non-Christian, literature is not always a good communications tool for that segment of our 'audience.' Even though most people can read at least a little, reading is so difficult for many of them that it becomes too difficult and therefore is often not done at all. The cassette simply requires the person to listen, which is easier and does not require nearly as much effort. There is also a time factor for the Christian who has to learn many new things. If reading is difficult in the first place, it takes a lot of time to re-read and re-read. During that time he cannot do anything else. The cassette, however, can play while he does many of this daily chores.

The Cassette Versus Radio

In most countries radio is too expensive to use in teaching scattered Christians, but no waste is encountered with cassettes in this regard. Radio requires people to listen at a specific time, while a cassette can be used at any convenient time. A radio does not repeat the message, but a cassette can repeat the same message 30 times if necessary. A radio program has to be designed for a large, varied audience, while a cassette can be tailored to a specific, limited segment. A radio station usually broadcasts programs in series, which is good, but all listeners have to begin following the series at the same time, or they will come in the middle of a series. A cassette teaching series can be started whenever needed, e.g., immediately after a person is converted.

Cassettes Versus Meetings and Personal Work

The new Christian may need to hear the same message again and again until it is understood, if his background is animism, or another totally different religion. This may mean he will have to listen dozens of times, requiring more time—and patience—than the missionary or pastor can spend.

Integrated Use of Cassettes

An integrated use of cassettes is the most effective use of them. The above comparisons do not in any way exclude the use of the other tools. We must use them together in an effective outreach.

During the research period such examples came up often. One family was first introduced to the Gospel through gospel records. Radio then reached the area. When they became Christians, cassettes were used in follow-up teaching. In a Christian hospital the staff skillfully use radio (over the PA system), cassettes and literature in an integrated ministry. Or, a church may rely on radio and literature in their outreach, then use cassettes for the teaching ministry.

The Cost of Cassettes in a Ministry to Christians

Although the cost involved in using cassettes may seem high, if all expenses are accounted for, it becomes one of the least expensive media. Just think of the many hours of playing time each cassette has in comparison to the cost of a pastor's time, a radio program, or a book. The hourly cost becomes minimal. If we thought only in terms of each person buying his own cassettes for personal use and playing them once or twice, then the cost would be very high. However, if people see the possibilities of a cassette ministry, the cassette programs are made to meet existing needs, and if the use of cassettes is explained, then the finance is also available.

It might be said here that most publishers who make cassettes available for sale in bookstores still have to see the need to explain the purpose of their cassettes, how to use them, where to use them, and what results can be expected if rightly used.

Communications Principles of the Cassette

The cassette is a personal medium or tool. It is used by a person to improve or expedite his or her work. In evangelistic outreach that person is usually a Christian, but in a ministry to Christians the user is generally the person himself. He uses it for his own spiritual growth. There exists a very high motivation and desire to learn. The cassette is used, not as an entertainment media like radio, but as a teaching media. It has no entertainment to compete with. If we program a cassette to compete with entertainment, we have missed the mark. Often cassettes are programmed as if they were designed for radio broadcasting, but actually radio and cassettes are totally different. The person plays the cassette because he wants to learn, and anything that does not fulfill that purpose is a distraction. Research and experience have proved these principles again and again, so we should not copy radio programs onto cassettes, as it was done in the beginning.

The cassette tool can be used by the person any time he wants it. Perhaps one person uses it while ironing clothes. One man, a blacksmith, plays the cassette all day long while working at the furnace preparing special axes. It is played by a man, lying on a sickbed; a business man, trying to catch up on his Bible studies, uses it while traveling in his car, and a family may gather round the cassette player in the living room. All of these people are INVOLVED. They are not just passive spectators. It is a cool communication that requires a lot of input from them.

RESEARCH NEEDED TO ESTABLISH
A BASIS FOR PROGRAMMING TO CHRISTIANS

Research is needed for a thorough understanding of the person the programs are made for. Among many things that must be considered are his cultural values, the social structure of his environment, his understanding of Christian concepts and of the Bible, his attitudes, his view of life as well as values, his religious background, and his financial status. Such knowledge is invaluable in programming. To meet a listener's need, you have to know and understand these needs. This will give you a basis and foundation for effective programming. When programming for the new Christian such points may be equally important.

Research will probably point out several different groups that may need special programming. Such differences may be due to education, background, or other things. There are also at least two different phases that must be considered—the new Christian and the more established Christian. (See figure 26.)

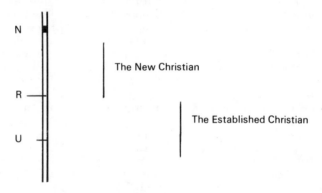

Figure 26
Target Audience for Programming

PROGRAMMING FOR THE NEW CHRISTIAN

Who Is He?

The first question we must ask is, "Who is the person that I'm going to reach and help with this production?" In the Christian life he is a new babe, but in life in general he is a grown-up. He does not live in a vacuum but in a complex society. He may not know very much about the Christian faith or the message of the Bible. He has grasped the outstretched hands of the Lord and received His salvation, but apart from that his understanding may include many misunderstandings. He may have been seriously affected by animistic beliefs, liberal thinking, or atheism, yet he is a newborn Christian who wants and needs to learn! He may come out of demon worship and at present be under almost constant attack from the evil one. He is at the same time searching and satisfied, joyous and terrified, open yet rejecting. He may be facing rejection from family and friends, or physical persecution.

What Does He Need?

Most of all he needs someone to take his hand, lead him on, and help him to walk. He may not be able to select the cassettes best suited to him, but the pastor or Christian friend can do that. As he is rejected by his old group, he has a big need for "belonging" and fellowship. He wants to learn to sing hymns. He needs assurance of faith and a firm foundation for his new outlook on life. He needs power to be victorious in the many immediate temptations and difficulties facing him. He needs help to share his testimony with others, but most of all he needs the Word. The message of the Bible is the keystone on which the new Christian's faith is founded. One Christian testified about the craving for the Word of God she experienced during her first days as a Christian, and a missionary told about how simple Bible readings and expositions helped many new Christians through these first difficult days.

How Can Cassettes Be Used
to Meet These Needs?

Before setting out to write the scripts and produce the programs for the cassettes, it is necessary to decide where and how the cassettes are going to be used. Are they going to be used in a group or by the person when he is alone? Will another Christian be present? (probably not). Is it going to be used in his home, in his car, or somewhere else? Though the use may differ from person to person, approximate answers to these questions should be sought and kept in mind during programming. The buyer or user of the cassette should be clearly instructed as to how it should be used.

Based on available experience and research, the following four types of cassette programs are suggested for the New Christian:

1. Evangelistic cassettes.
2. Singing cassettes.
3. Basic teaching series.
4. A book study on the Life of Christ.

1. *The evangelistic cassette.* It may sound strange that an evangelistic cassette is suggested for the new Christian, but there are several reasons for this suggestion. There is a good chance that the new Christian still needs to reaffirm his decision—a post-decision reaffirmation to himself and to others. He will also immediately have opportunities to witness to those friends and relatives who see the change in his life. A well-prepared evangelistic cassette which both teaches the new Christian and witnesses to others can be of great value in these first days and weeks. It may be a good idea to let one or two such cassettes stay with him for a considerable length of time.

The program should be easily followed, encouraging and joyous. It should be bold in presentation and inspiring in faith. It must be positive and in good taste. Such a cassette may very well open up not only the one new home, but many other homes and hearts to the Gospel. However, if the cassette is poorly done and in bad taste, it could close these same hearts and homes, resulting in harm for the cause of Christ as well as for the new Christian it is supposed to help. The program cannot, therefore, be preaching as such but a friendly presentation of the new Life in Christ, telling what it means to a person to have entered this Way.

The new Christian has some new friends—the people who speak on the cassette—and he is bringing these new friends along with him to his 'old friends' and family. Everything on the cassette should be done and said in such a manner as it would be said and done if the speakers were actually with him in that home or living room. Their manners will either turn them on or off! The voices should be those of common men and women who have found something wonderful. They have found new life in Christ.

Usually the cassette will play for 30 minutes on each side. The program outline shown on figure 27 can be suggested for one side, or it can be expanded to cover both sides of the cassette.

2. *Singing cassettes.* Another very important cassette that will also be highly treasured by the new Christian

1. Introductory, light instrumental music. Main purpose is to call attention to the introduction.   1.00 min.
2. Introduction and a 'chatty' interview with a Christian in which he shares what it means to him to be a Christian.   4.00 min.
3. A hymn the interviewee likes. He has told why he likes it.   2.30 min.
4. Short message explaining the way of salvation in easy, sharing terms. Care should be taken to base this on scripture verses. The reference to each verse should be given.   5.00 min.
5. A 'testimony-hymn.' A popular hymn should be chosen.   3.30 min.
6. Short introduction to the next hymn.   1.10 min.
7. Hymn. Preferably a call to trust in Christ.   2.00 min.
8. Introduction to another Christian who is going to share some more.   1.00 min.
9. This Christian tells what goes on in a church, why they go to church, and gives his own testimony which should include a desire to tell others what Christ can do.   6.00 min.
10. Congregational singing. (lively).   4.00 min.
     Total   30.00 min.

Figure 27
Outline of Script for Evangelistic Cassette
To Be Used by a New Christian

is a singing cassette. Singing and music cassettes can generally be made in such a way that a wide 'audience' can use them.

The new Christian has become a member of a new group. Since he probably feels totally rejected by his old group, he has a strong urge or desire to be really integrated into the new group, to be 'one of them.' Singing helps him in this regard. If he is able to sing along in church, he can express his feelings and devotions with the other Christians in the worship service. There is probably also a vacuum in his life which can be filled by Christian singing. This can be a witness to others at the same time.

Hymns for a cassette should be carefully selected, not just a hodgepodge of everything. There should be some of the commonly used evangelistic songs that the new Christian probably has heard and was drawn by. He will like to sing these again and again. The cassette should also include some of the hymns that are most frequently used in the church services; hymns that are loved and cherished by Christians everywhere; hymns that speak to the heart; hymns that express the deep devotion and love of the heart to God.

The hymns on a cassette for a new Christian should be easy to learn. It is advisable to select as many local or ethnic tunes as possible. If the local music is the five-tone scale, and the translated hymns are set to the Western seven-tone scale, the chances are that it may take months before he can sing along, and feel comfortable with it.

On the other hand, if local tunes are used, he can learn all the hymns you can put on a cassette in one week or less. Such hymns communicate to him in a language and tune he understands and is able to imitate and identify with in a way he cannot do with traditional Western hymns. This was the single point that was emphasized most often by both missionaries and local Christians during research interviews in Thailand, and it has been emphasized equally strong in interviews with people from other countries and cultures as well. As a further example it has been pointed out that an African composer will copyright the rhythm rather than the melody, because rhythm is the most important part of his music.

When producing a cassette for a new Christian, it should be remembered that the purpose is not entertainment, but teaching and fellowship. It is, therefore, of little use to record elaborate choir recitals or four-part harmony. A professional singer may not meet the need either. That does not mean that we should not use professional singers and musicians. The main guidelines are simplicity and clarity. This may not always satisfy music directors and teachers, but they will communicate to the new Christians. Solo voices are best, but a small group can be used if it is clear and expressive. The instrumental accompaniment should encourage the new Christian to sing along with the cassette. The quality of recording and production must be kept at a professional level if at all possible.

The hymnbook situation is generally a cause of confusion in most countries, for each denomination or mission is producing its own hymnbooks. On the mission fields some groups publish hymnbooks that look like exact copies of the ones used in their home countries. Often several editions exist of each hymnbook. This may not cause difficulties in the United States with the millions of Christians, but in a country with only 30,000 Christians, it is a major problem for the recording studio and radio broadcaster. A partial solution is to avoid using hymns from different hymnbooks on the same cassette. A different cassette should be produced for each hymnbook. This may sometimes call for more than one recording of the same hymn if several versions are in use. There is no other way to overcome the problem unless the major denominations and missions agree on common hymnbooks!

While producing the program, it should be remembered that people are trying to sing along and may be following in their own hymnbooks. If all hymns in a small hymnbook are recorded and the hymns follow the same order on the cassette, there is no real problem, but in most cases this is not possible. People must be given time to find the hymn in their hymnbooks without having to stop the cassette. It becomes too bothersome if they have to stop the cassette every time. Between the hymns the name of the hymnbook, number of the next hymn, and the title of the hymn should be given, then repeated. This may take 10 to 15 seconds, but the listener can use this time to find the hymn in his own book. Those who are unable to read still need time to mentally change from one tune to another. The part of a script, shown in figure 28, is included to illustrate how the singing cassette for a new Christian can be made.

3. *Basic Bible teaching series*. It cannot be taken for granted that the new Christian clearly understands the essential Christian doctrines. He probably needs some general knowledge of the Bible. This will give him a basic foundation for his new faith and give him the ability to answer questions usually asked by non-Christians.

The material on these cassettes needs to be easy. It has been found that some good children's material can be used as program material for the new Christian. It is of no use to enter into controversies or difficulties at this point, for this would just confuse the listener. The teaching must be positive and encouraging, made so that a family can listen together if they want to. A systematic treatment of the basic Christian concepts will be a good way to proceed. At the Voice of Peace a set of 9 cassettes was built on the Thai edition of Ken Taylor's book, *Devotions for the Children's Hour.*[1]

ANNOUNCER:
The hymnbook used for this cassette is the new edition of *Hymns of the Christian Life*, which is published by the C.M.A. Literature Department. We invite you to sing along as we sing some of these great hymns. The first one is number 12, "Great Is Thy Faithfulness." Number 12 in the *Hymns of the Christian Life*.
HYMN: "Great Is Thy Faithfulness."

ANNOUNCER:
The next hymn we are going to sing from *Hymns of the Christian Life* is number 190 and the title of the hymn is, "My Hope Is Built on Nothing Less." The number is 190, "My Hope Is Built on Nothing Less."
HYMN: "My Hope Is Built on Nothing Less."
etc. etc.

Figure 28
Example of Script for Singing Cassette

It goes through 48 aspects of the Christian faith and includes such topics as: "Who Is God? Death and Resurrection of Christ, the Bible, Sin and Forgiveness, Prayer, Who are the Angels? etc.

The production should take into account that the listener may not listen long at one time, so if short spaces are left between 'programs' there will be time to turn the player off and then continue the listening later.

Identification is a key word, so every attempt should be made to make it possible for the intended listener to relate to the voices on the cassette. It may be helpful to have two or three voices, but each voice should be taking the same part in each program.

The outline given in figure 29 was used for the teaching set at Voice of Peace. This format has been quite good, yet the use of Bible reading as the first part of the program has been questioned as a number of people have difficulties in understanding the reading.

Each such program may be 10 to 15 minutes in length. Unlike the evangelistic and singing cassettes, these teaching cassettes should be with the user only one or two

1. Short Bible reading. Give the passage and then read slowly and clearly.	2.00 min.
2. An easy explanation of this passage, applying it in some way to the daily life of the Christian.	4.00 min.
3. One or two questions can be asked on the passage or subject, and they are then answered by the speaker.	2.00 min.
4. Short prayer.	1.00 min.
5. Hymn, specially selected for the text or topic if possible. Give number in hymnbook and maybe a couple of introductory comments. If it is a chorus, then read it first.	3.00 min.
	12.00 min.

Figure 29

Outline of Basic Bible Teaching Script for the New Christian

weeks, as we want him to proceed quickly through this basic series.

4. *Book study on the life of Christ.* The Basic Teaching series should give an all-round knowledge of the Christian faith, but the new Christian also needs to learn how to study and apply the message directly from the Bible. The aim of this series is to give an overall picture of the life of Christ.

The study could be based on a harmony of the Gospels, but it may be better to base it on one single book. Most Christian workers have usually begun teaching the Gospel of John, but this may not always be the best choice. In some countries the Gospel of Mark may be more immediately relevant. In non-Christian cultures, a study of the first chapter of Genesis should be given before the study of the Gospels in order to give perspective to the study.

Most of the available cassettes that aim at teaching have been recorded in churches before live audiences. This method does not suit our purpose. For to be effective, the speaker or teacher on the cassette must act and speak as if he is sitting in a living room alone with one person, explaining the Scriptures to him and showing him how these passages relate to his daily life. Therefore, the main qualification for the teacher, or scriptwriter, is experience. He must have experience in working with the type of people who will be using the cassette. He must be able to relate in a personal way to the individual, making applications as he proceeds through the lesson.

It is best to concentrate the teaching in short sections, but the length of the sections should be governed by the time a subject needs rather than a time schedule. The series should not be longer than 5 to 6 cassettes (5 to 6 hours).

The teaching must inspire the new Christian so that he will study the Bible by himself and apply it to his own life. One experienced missionary was quoted as saying, "The cassette can do more and better work than I can do in 3 months of Bible teaching."

Generally speaking, we should stay away from using missionary speakers, and concentrate on national voices. On teaching cassettes for Christians, a missionary might sometimes be used as speaker if his language is excellent and if his experience and skill justify using him. The main criteria is to use a 'trustworthy' voice, the voice of an experienced man who the listener can look up to and learn from.

PROGRAMMING FOR THE ESTABLISHED CHRISTIAN

In the section above the concern was with the new Christian, or the first six months of his Christian experience. This does not mean that many established Christians would not also profit from using these same cassettes. It is a sad fact that many have not progressed beyond the earliest stages of Christian development. Our research will have given us much information about the "average" Christian and his needs. He may have been a Christian for only six months or he may look back on many years of Christian life. He may never have been effective in his witness to another person, yet he has friends whom he wants to win for Christ. He may be afraid to witness as he fears the implications, not being able to answer questions the other person may ask. His life may not have been too victorious either, and maybe some temptations have been too strong for him. He may be desiring a part in the ministry of the church, yet feels incompetent and inferior to other church members. His devotions may not have been as they should be. On the other hand, there will be those who have been victorious, have been witnessing, and have been serving, yet feel the need for further study and encouragement.

The needs of the Christian will almost certainly not be met by cassettes alone, but many of them can be met if the cassettes are really produced for these specific purposes. The needs are in the devotional area, such as being inspired to witness for Christ. He needs to study how to answer the questions that non-Christians will ask him, so he can be effective in his testimony. He needs to get further into the study of the Word, so he will progress on to maturity and victory. The results seen in Thailand and other places when such needs are met by cassettes give boldness and hope in believing that great changes can and will take place in the church worldwide as we learn to use the cassettes in effective ministry.

Like many farmers, Jeng found it very difficult to read. Many of the words and concepts used—even in the Bible—were beyond his understanding and experience. The teaching cassettes came to his help and within a very short time this man amazed the missionary by the insight he had. This insight and understanding was expressed in prayers as well as in his testimony. When Jeng witnessed he often used the points from the cassettes, but he translated them into his own dialect and way of speaking.

Another missionary reported that in each of eight places where he had placed cassette players, there was great spiritual growth evident within a short time.

A Christian lady whose husband was a drunkard experienced a complete change in her attitudes after receiving teaching by cassette—and in the process her two teenage daughters listened and both accepted Christ as their Savior.

The four following categories of cassettes are suggested for the ministry to Christians:

1. Question and answer.
2. Singing and music.
3. Teaching series.
4. Devotional series.

1. *Question and answer cassettes.* The Apostle Peter writes that we should always be ready to give an answer for the faith that is in us, yet experience shows that the lack of ability to answer basic questions about the Christian

107

message has paralyzed evangelistic efforts again and again. The Christian needs to learn how to answer the questions that he will receive so that there will be a positive outcome.

These questions may not be the ones generally raised in a theological seminary, neither should they be answered that way. The best way to collect the questions is to interview twenty or more Christians and ask what kind of questions they receive from non-believers. Also, questions received in radio response can be collected, and direct interviews with non-Christians done to find out why they are not Christians. Generally, the questions are almost always the same or very similar in nature. Then select the most common 10 to 15 questions to be answered on a cassette. Evangelists, missionaries, and pastors will also know what subjects are often misunderstood. These can form the basis for other suitable questions.

The next step is to select the person or persons to answer the questions. Time will be needed to work out clear, concise, and effective answers, which will not only satisfy the inquirer but will also point him to Christ. This should all be in script form (all cassette material should be) so that checking and rewriting can be done. Each question and answer should then be pretested with several people before actual production.

During production at least two voices should be used. One voice will ask the question the same way with the same intonations as the non-Christian would ask it. The teacher then answers the question—brief, clear, and effective. Some answers may be very brief, but generally they should be less than five minutes long.

If such a cassette is played in a group of Christians and non-Christians, an identification and polarization is achieved. The non-Christian will identify with the one asking the questions, and the Christian will identify with the teacher. In the process of listening the Christian is taught how to answer in a live situation, and an effective evangelistic outreach is achieved at the same time. In effectiveness, no other cassettes have given better results than question and answer cassettes, and only singing cassettes have had better sales. It came up again and again during interviews that the Christians not only used these cassettes, but they soon remembered the answers by heart. They used the material constantly in their witness and ministry. The apostle Paul argued in the market place[2] and so the question and answer cassettes help local Christians to do the same.

2. *Singing and music.* A wide variety of cassettes with singing and music will help the Christian. Some will be to teach the same singing as for new Christians, but with more and different types of hymns. Some churches sing along with these cassettes during their services. For the more established Christian there may also be a need for more elaborate types of recordings, including choir recitals and special music. Such recordings will be more for his enjoyment than for teaching.

3. *Teaching series.* Most Christians need more teaching than they get in their churches. The statistics on how few books Christians read are startling; some never read even a single volume. The need for further teaching is enormous, but the cassette can help to change that situation. Many cassettes on the market that aim at meeting this need are almost always recorded at a church service and so lack much of the input that should be given to a cassette production. It is important for church leaders to make sure that their cassette libarary is built up effectively so that there is a reasonable systematic continuity from cassette to cassette, not just all the same kind of material.

Suggestions as to what material can be used are endless. There can be studies on specific books of the Bible, on special topics, on the Christian life, etc. A list of the most important topics should be compiled, then make an effort to buy or produce cassettes that will speak on them. Each series or set can be from one to five or six cassettes, but not more.

A number of cassettes on special topics is necessary for any cassette library or project. Included will be such topics as: Stewardship, Prayer, Joy, Witnessing, and Fellowship. The cassette should not just be a sermon or a collection of unrelated bits and pieces without any specific order. It should have not only direct teaching, but also a persuasive goal that will aim at changing the listeners attitude and behavior in the direction of the teaching.

First of all, the subject should be studied carefully. Do people really need teaching on the subject? Why? What are the difficulties they face? Talk to people about their problems concerning this topic. Collect testimonies from others. Select hymns on the subject. Study the Bible passages relating to the subject. Then, with a definite listener in mind and with specific objectives, set out to write the script. A scenario of a 30-minute program on the subject of Joy might look something like figure 30.

1. Music. "Joyous."	app. 1.00 min.
2. A testimony, or a dramatic episode from a testimony.	app. 4.00 min.
3. Instrumental music-bridge (to give time for the impression of the testimony to sink in).	app 2.00 min.
4. A few questions are raised as to why some Christians don't always have joy.	app. 3.00 min.
5. A panel of 2 laymen and 1 or 2 pastors answer these questions from experience and from the Bible.	app. 9.00 min.
6. A hymn about Joy.	app. 3.00 min.
7. Short message. Challenge to the listener on how to be joyful.	app. 6.00 min.
8. Instrumental-meditating music.	app. 2.00 min.
	30.00 min.

Figure 30
Teaching the Subject of Joy

For this type of cassette program a 'preacher' should not be used. Everything has to be kept on a 'sharing' basis. It is a friend sharing with a fellow-believer how he can experience Joy, or the blessing of giving. If some kind of specific commitment is called for on the cassette, it may add to the effectiveness of the program.

4. *Devotional series.* So far most of the types of cassettes that have been mentioned have been designed to be played at home or in private. The devotional cassettes are more for churches, small groups, or prayer meetings. Even though the Christians may be receiving devotional help in church, there is often a need for the special inspiration and uplift that can be gained from another speaker. Many such cassettes are on the market. In countries where there are many scattered Christian groups with no pastors and with little teaching and preaching available, such devotional cassettes may cause critical changes in the church's life and outreach. Devotional cassettes are usually in the form of preaching and will most likely be listened

to only once or twice. They are then passed on to another group or returned to the library. Due to the short life cycle of such a cassette and higher production cost, care must be given to the selection of speakers.

THE INTEGRATION OF A
CASSETTE PROJECT WITH THE
CHURCH MINISTRY

Because cassettes are tools to be used by people, they can be enormously effective with intelligent use. They do not supplant the church ministry, but they supplement it. When building a cassette project or library, whether from the production and programming point of view or from a buyer's point of view, it is important to carefully review each cassette and see where it fits into the total ministry. The church or mission should establish a cassette library so that there are cassettes for each needed purpose. The purpose of each individual cassette should be carefully explained to each church member and worker, so that an orderly use of cassettes may be implemented. This concerns not only cassettes for Christians, but also cassettes for evangelism.

One church is recording the Sunday sermons and choir numbers in order to extend the effect of the service. Orders for cassettes are taken after the service, and they are then mailed out two days later. For shut-ins the cassettes are delivered in person and supplied free of charge, but otherwise the cost is $2.25 for each C60 cassette. Many other churches are doing the same, and some are using high-speed duplicating facilities that enable them to sell the cassettes at the door as people leave the church. The church mentioned above also sends some cassettes air mail to their missionaries. The effect of a recorded church service has been quite good for members, who want a repetition of the message, and for shut-ins who cannot come to church as usual, but the effect in terms of evangelistic outreach has been very limited.

111

CHAPTER 6

Programming Cassettes
for Evangelism

Evangelism generally refers to all the work that takes place before conversion and includes leading the person to Christ. It includes all the areas of sowing and part of the reaping area of our model. The term "Church Growth" has been used a lot during the last few years, but often it has been used almost interchangeably with the term evangelism. To achieve real church growth, we must have a total program which fulfills all the aspects of the Great Commission: sowing, reaping, and refining. Real church growth, therefore, includes more than evangelism. The area of concern in this particular chapter is the area which is generally understood as evangelism. It can be illustrated on the model as shown on figure 31.

The aim of evangelism is to lead a person to Christ, but this work has two phases, sowing and reaping. The goal of sowing is not salvation, but the goal of reaping is. Sowing attempts to spread the Word, help it take root, grow up, and ripen. The ready harvest is then the object of the reaping aspect of our work.

CASSETTES AND EVANGELISM

The stated objective of most cassette producers in Christian circles is often evangelism, but after close evaluation

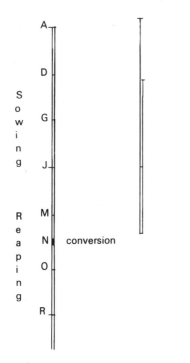

Evangelism: A-N
Sowing: A-J
Reaping: J-R

Evangelistic use of cassettes:
Sowing: app. E-J
Reaping: app. J-N

Figure 31
Evangelistic Cassettes

the actual aim of the cassettes seems to be going in a different direction. The main problem in using cassettes for evangelism is to get the cassettes into the non-Christian's home so he can listen to them. He probably will not buy them himself. If cassettes are to be used in evangelism, they must be brought to the intended listener by a Christian. It is the testimony of a Christian that opens the door for the use of cassettes. This might have been the result of personal follow-up of a contact made through evangelistic radio broadcasting. In a few cases, responses have come through the mail requesting cassettes, but these are the few. The situation is such that cassettes cannot usually aim at reaching the man at points A or B on the model, but rather someone who has already had some exposure. In evangelism the cassette is a tool that helps the Christian to expand and improve his ministry. For the general sowing of the Word to the masses, radio and television have much better capabilities. Cassettes come in at a later stage. There are some notable exceptions to that rule, though. It has, for example, been found that a Muslim who will not listen to a Christian giving his testimony will attentively listen to the cassette, even if the speaker sits next to him. The cassettes have opened up Muslim areas for the Gospel this way.

RESEARCH

It cannot be overemphasized that it is of utmost importance that we understand the listener and his environment. Programming cassettes for evangelism is a sensitive matter. The spiritual segmentation research mentioned earlier will give much information, but it is even more important to know the listener's understanding of Christian concepts, his attitudes to Christians and God, his interests in life, and so on. The importance of each of these areas will vary from program to program, from purpose to purpose.

To illustrate this point we can again look at the situation in Thailand. Information has been compiled from direct interviewing, articles and books published by anthropologists and linguists, and from writings by Thai authors. Only a couple of words are explained briefly to show the understanding and connotative meaning of religious words used by the average Thai citizen.

The word used for God is "PraChaw," The word is used as a title for the king and as a name for Buddha. The first part of the word "Pra" may be used for 'god,' a Buddhist monk, or an image. When referring to deity, the word PraChaw does not carry the concept of a living, personal God.

In general the Thai accept that Christ is a good teacher like Buddha, but they object to the exculsive claims of Christ. Christ is the supreme teacher of the foreigner's (Westerner's) religion. The love of Christ and His vicarious death is a puzzle to most Thai, but His resurrection power is intriguing.

Many other words could be mentioned such as sin, faith, salvation, heaven, and religion, which all carry different connotative meanings. Apart from religious connotations, the cultural situation also influences the understanding of Christian terminology. Take, for example. the term "God our Father." The whole family concept and fatherhood is understood differently in the Thai culture.

Such research data, together with experience obtained by the use of a variety of cassettes and approaches, form the basis for the programming guidelines suggested in the following. Information from different cultures and sources has also been utilized. The type of programs suggested are those that have proved effective.

PROGRAMMING TO THE NON-CHRISTIAN

The available programs that meet the requirements we must set for evangelistic programming is so far very limited. Even in Christian radio, which has been around for many years, the vast majority of broadcasts are programmed for Christians. The experimentation and experience on which we can build our principles for evangelistic cassettes is limited, so Christian communicators should be encouraged to begin serious experimentation and production of truly evangelistic material.

It is important for the producer to understand the listener and his environment. Communication must be established through "frequencies" and channels he is tuned in to. Don't just preach, but ask some questions. The listener should not just sit passively, but he should be engaged in the communication so that he is actively thinking about the subject. This may be obtained by asking rhetorical questions, or by having another voice—one that the listener can identify with—asking the questions on the cassette.

Jesus asked a lot of rhetorical questions in His ministry too! The message on the cassette must be friendly and positive, and it should be straightforward without any attempt to hide anything. It always helps to smile when you enter somebody's home, so the cassette should start on a happy, joyful note. Some productions talk about Christians and the church negatively with the idea that they will, in this way, gain the interest of the listener. This is a mistake. Any cassette that is negative toward the church or Christians will be accepted as hypocritical, and

115

the message has a good chance of being screened out or rejected. You cannot sell a product and at the same time criticize the results of this product. Be positive and friendly.

INTEGRATION WITH GENERAL OUTREACH

In evangelism the cassette ministry must be integrated with the general outreach of the church. In this way it will expand and strengthen that ministry. Interest generated by radio programs may be followed up by cassettes. The personal worker may multiply the impact of his work by using cassettes. A church or mission that establishes a cassette library, which is coordinated and systematized, will greatly improve the effectiveness of the ministry of its individual members.

PROBLEMS INVOLVED IN TRANSLATING WESTERN EVANGELISTIC MATERIAL INTO OTHER LANGUAGES AND CULTURES

Many missionaries and Christian workers are asking for scripts to be translated. The problem of translation concerns literature and radio as well as cassettes. The following quotation from Dr. Nida is relevant:

> What makes even less sense is the tendency for popular Christian radio programs in the United States to spend considerable sums of money getting such messages translated, or in some instances poorly adapted, to foreign language audiences. The results are pathetically meager in terms of such expenditures involved. What is needed is the creative development of local programs at home and abroad which can communicate not merely through words but also through effective music, drama, and indigenous art.[1]

Recently a number of interviews were conducted with Christian workers from seven different Asian countries and a number of missionaries. It was evident from the interviews that there was a negative attitude to the idea of translating evangelistic material to Asian languages. Most of the evangelistic materials used in Asian countries have been translated from Western material. Now there is a marked tendency to concentrate on translating material for Christians only, and to write and develop evangelistic material in the country where it is to be used.

Some of the basic difficulties involved in translating evangelistic material were found to be: making the translation culturally acceptable, adapting to their way of thinking, giving differences of connotative meaning of words and terms, and in the misunderstanding of concepts. Also some ideas and illustrations are irrelevant, values and needs are different, and there were difficulties involved in finding qualified translators.

If a translation is attempted, it should not be literal. Something might be left out sometimes, while in other places an explanation of the text may be necessary. Illustrations should be changed or adapted, and expressions and concepts must be translated into the Oriental or African way of thinking. Obviously, most evangelistic material published in the West is not translated on this basis.

The question is still, Why do missionaries translate evangelistic material? Often there is lack of talent and qualified teachers. However, a personal interview with a missionary, who was in charge of a literature agency in an Asian country for years, revealed that the main criteria used is often finance. Funds are limited and they are often approached by an American organization who wants *their* material translated and are willing to pay for it.

SOWING BY CASSETTE

Cassettes may be used in many more types of situations than mentioned here, but the examples given in this handbook are limited to those which have actually worked in real situations. The aim of cassettes for sowing is not soul winning (reaping), but preparing a harvest. The programming of a cassette will be influenced by the situation in which it is used and the cultural variables.

In some cultures people respond readily on an emotional level, while a cognitive appeal is more effective in other countries. A missionary with years of experience in Thailand said, "The Thai want to know, to understand, to have facts. They want to understand some of the principles and basics of Christianity before they accept the Lord, so an outline of the main teaching of Christianity becomes very

117

evangelistic." Such information is very valuable for evangelistic programming.

The classification of "sowing" cassettes are in the following based on how they are used.

1. Cassettes used by a Christian while he is present.
2. Cassettes used by a Christian in his own home.
3. Cassettes left with an interested person.
4. Cassettes used over a hospital or public PA system.

Cassettes Used by a Christian
While He Is Present

So far, this has been the most common use of evangelistic cassettes. A Christian plays it for his relatives or neighbors, or he may go to another village to witness to distant relatives. The cassette is the tool he takes along. There may be only one or two people with him around the cassette player, or there may be a whole group of neighbors and relatives. The testimony of the Christian is the most important single factor, but the cassette assists and reinforces him in that task.

Or perhaps it is a suburban housewife who has been witnessing to a neighbor over a cup of coffee. Now she plays a cassette for her neighbor. Evangelistic cassettes can be used by Christians almost everywhere. There are many testimonies to this fact.

The evangelistic cassette for the new Christian, and the question and answer cassettes for the established Christians are both designed for sowing. Often the singing cassettes will also be good sowing tools. The reader is adviced to re-read the section on these cassettes.

Cassettes Used by a Christian
in His Own Home

Many neighbors and relatives are often exposed to the gospel message by a cassette player, which a new Christian has brought into his home. The effect is multiplied in tropical countries where walls are thin and windows only have screens. As the new Christian listens to the teaching, his family also listens.

A young girl became a Christian while she worked as a cook for some missionaries. Later she went home to live with her parents in the village. She brought the cassettes along, and it did not take long before the repetitious teaching was accepted by her father. He, too, became a Christian. Her mother was antagonistic at first but later expressed a desire to be a Christian. Although illiterate, she has memorized most of the cassettes. The girl's brother, who spent much of his time drinking, suddenly said one day, after listening to the teaching, "I want to become a Christian." He had not received other witness. That young man's life was changed completely, and he has been growing in the faith.

Thus the cassette in the home of a Christian has often changed antagonism into interest, and interest into faith. The cassettes used are generally the same as those programmed for the new Christian.

Cassettes Left with an Interested Person

This environment and situation is quite different. The person, who probably is alone, is interested in the Gospel, things he doesn't understand, and wants to find out about them. A friend has left him a cassette. This situation leaves no competition from the entertainment media or any other source. If the listener should be a housewife, she is probably doing something else while listening. A man may be listening while driving home from work. If there is interest enough to listen to the cassette in the first place, we can count on a learning motivation so the person will be attentive to the message presented. The teaching cassette must be able to convey the basic concepts of the Christian faith, especially the concept of God (who He is), the concept of man (a sinner in need of Christ), and the concept of salvation (the way of Christ).

Because it is expected that the person will be listening by himself, the cassette must be completely self-explanatory. Of course, if the cassette was brought there by a friend, there will be follow-up when he returns to get the cassette. The teaching would be easier and more effective if some other means could be used at the same time, but this is not possible. Therefore if effective teaching is to take place, we have to engage more than the ears of the listener. He has to use his mental capabilities, too. Fortunately the cassette offers some unique possibilities to achieve this. Creative and skillful programming will be required, and we can learn much from programmed instruction material, from correspondence courses for nonbelievers, and from other sound media.

It is expected that the producer of such cassettes will have first gained a thorough knowledge of the listener and his environment. The next step will be to select the points or subjects that we want to teach this interested person. If some good correspondence courses are available, they may help us to get the outline down. The scenario given in figure 32 will give an idea of how the script can be built up.

This kind of structure is programmed teaching by cassette, and on such a cassette or two you can effectively teach the basic concepts of the Bible to an interested person. The programming should be made in such a way that it progresses logically.

1. INSTRUCTIONS: On this cassette we want to share with you what Christianity is really about. After each point a question is asked. If you do not know the answer to that question, stop the cassette while the music is played and think about it. Then start the cassette again to see if you came up with the correct answer.   app.   .20 min.

2. Some information is given. This may or may not include a Bible verse.   1.00 min.

3. A simple question on the subject.   .10 min.

4. Instrumental music.   .10 min.

5. The answer to the last question.   .15 min.

6. Information.   1.00 min.

7. Question   .10 min.

8. Music.   .10 min.

9. Answer.   .15 min.

10. Information.   1.00 min.
     etc. etc.

Figure 32
Programmed Bible Teaching
for the non-Christian

In later questions you can build on information given earlier as well. The reasons for this type of teaching are many. One is that good teaching principles are followed.

By asking questions, the listener is engaged in the communication, and he really tries to work out an answer for himself. Of course it is not expected that most people will stop the cassette and think. That is the reason for the short pause with music. The music, the pause and the knowledge that he ought to stop, all make him attentive to the answer—that is really the main purpose. When a person has listened through such a cassette a few times, he will have a basic understanding of the Christian faith.

Such programmed teaching cassettes can be used almost everywhere—in affluent churches as well as primitive rural groups—and the same principles can be followed. Only the level of information and the difficulty of the questions will change. By using teaching cassettes before reaping is attempted, the chances of a lasting fruit are multiplied many times. As Jesus said in the parable of the Sower: he understood, and received, and bore hundredfold fruit.

Cassettes Used over a Hospital
or Public PA System

Most Christian hospitals have PA systems that broadcast into the rooms and corridors of the entire hospital. This has been a tremendous boost to the general evangelistic outreach of the medical ministry. Due to easier operation, some hospitals have begun using cassettes instead of tapes or direct reception of Christian radio programs. When cassettes are broadcast in the same way as radio programs and the listeners hear the program only once, then there is really no difference from radio broadcasting. Cassettes for this purpose can, therefore, be produced in the same way as good evangelistic radio programs, or cassette copies of such programs can be made. The hospital may need further tapes with music or special programs, but the communications principles involved are exactly the same as for radio broadcasting. The only difference is that the audience is a captive audience and Christian workers are around.

It is beyond the scope of this book to go into details of how a radio program is programmed; but it should be remembered that in radio programming there must be some entertainment, for the listener will probably be doing something else at the same time, and he will only listen once to the same message. A person who has become interested through broadcasting over the PA system in a hospital can be followed up and led on effectively by cassettes.

The hospital patients and his relatives waiting with him (in some countries day and night) have time to listen again and again to the cassettes. To sum up, treat broadcasting cassettes as broadcasting, but the follow-up cassette as cassette ministry. This plan is already used by many Christian hospitals.

REAPING BY CASSETTE

In the same way that radio and television are not good reaping tools, so cassettes are not good reaping tools in themselves, but they are very effective in the hands of the reaper. They can help immensely to give that challenge or stimulus needed to call a person to accept Christ.

Many cassettes on sale in Western bookstores indicate that the producers think non-Christians will go to a Christian bookstore, buy a cassette, and listen to a program which is similar to a church revival meeting. The cassettes are supposed to do the whole job themselves. This probably won't happen. It is very difficult to produce cassettes that can do it all by themselves. In the hands of a Christian, however, a wide variety of cassettes can be used. Some evangelistic cassettes which are actual recordings from meetings (such as Billy Graham meetings) can be used, but it is better if the programs are produced specifically for cassettes. Messages made for the living room are more effective on cassette than those recorded at a large stadium or cathedral.

Earlier in this book it was suggested that films and evangelistic meetings be concentrated around the reaping ministry. Some experimentation was made in Thailand concerning the use of cassettes in the reaping ministry. Films are expensive to produce, so it was desired to look for another visual that would be cheaper to produce and use. Attempts were made to produce soundtracks on cassettes for posters and pictures. These were all used quite effectively, yet the use has not been wide enough to give a realistic report.

Then a series of four stories were produced on slides. They were each illustrated cartoon style on 10 or 11 slides. The art, script, and production were all done by a Thai, and the stories included a good portion of Thai humor. A dramatic soundtrack with plenty of sound effects was put on a cassette. Each story lasted 12-13 minutes, and all four stories were combined on a single C60 cassette. The result was four audio visual presentations costing just a few dollars, compared to hundreds of dollars for films.

It is not suggested that they are equally effective to films, but simply that they are effective. The second time one of the sets was shown was in a prison where an inmate received Christ as a direct result of the challenge from this simple slide/cassette cartoon. The sets are easy to use, cheap to buy, and easy to produce, so they do suggest that effective audio visuals can be produced at a cost the less affluent churches can afford.

FOLLOW-UP TO EVANGELISTIC CASSETTES

If evangelistic cassettes are used by themselves, by selling them in a bookstore, then follow-up is not easy. On the other hand, if they are used in the context of a total communications program, then it is almost irrelevant to discuss the subject of follow-up. It is already there. When evangelistic efforts have succeeded and a person accepts Christ, it is important to remember that the Great Commission includes more—there is still some way to point Z on the model.

After a person becomes a Christian, cassettes are most effective. The first few days in the life of a new Christian are very important. The lasting fruit of evangelism often depends on how we help him during that time. One missionary, who works in an area of animism and demon worship, mentioned that he always tries to get a cassette player to a new Christian the very same day he is converted. Just listening to the Word is an enormous help to the new Christian in his attempt to withstand the counterattacks from the evil one. Much prayer is also needed.

CHAPTER 7

Programming Cassettes for Lay-Leadership-Training

THE GREAT NEED FOR LAY-LEADERSHIP-TRAINING

Qualified leadership in the church is of utmost importance. Many a church has either advanced or gone into extinction simply because of the quality of leadership it had. The apostle Paul realized the need for good leadership in his ministry, so towards the end of his ministry one of his major concerns was for Timothy to install good leaders in the church and then train them. "And the things which you have heard from me in the presence of many witnesses, these entrust to faithful men, who will be able to teach others also." [1] The very concept of the church includes leadership at various levels. The Bible also tells us that these leaders must be spiritual men who are able to teach others also. [2]

Figure 33 indicates the approximate position of lay leaders on the spiritual segmentation model.

Present Position of Many Christian Groups

The traditional approach to leadership training has centered around the training of a few pastors, but has largely forgotten the training of lay leaders. This approach has led to the sad situation in some countries where most churches have no trained leaders at all. The pastors are too few and the churches cannot afford to pay them. In our eagerness to multiply members, we may have neglected the "refining" part of the Great Commission. With the possibility of a worldwide awakening, this problem presents itself as the most important challenge to the church today.

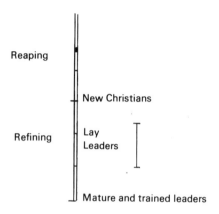

Figure 33
Position of Lay Leaders on Spiritual Segmentation Model

Potential of Trained Leaders

It may be needless to elaborate on this point, but the great potential of a church with well-trained lay leaders must be mentioned. These same points give great potential to a cassette training program.

The Church will be given spiritual food.
The Church will be led in evangelism.
The Church will be having a testimony in the community.
The Church will be self-supporting.

Changes Caused by Extension Programs

An encouraging change is being felt in leadership training methods and objectives around the world. This change is mainly due to the theories of education by extension. A lay-leadership-training program using cassettes follows many of the same principles. The main philosophy of extension is that education should be "person-centered" rather than "institution-centered." Instead of bringing the students to the institution (the education), the institution must be brought to the student. This must be done at the educational level of the students, in their own environment. The word extension has in this context been explained as:

1. *Geographical extension.* The institution brings the education to the place where the student is.

2. *Extension of time.* Study schedules are set up after the student has been asked when he can study. Maybe 5:30 a.m.!

3. *Cultural extension.* The student studies within his own subculture.

4. *Academic extension.* The academic level of the extension teaching depends on the academic level of the people in the pews. This may mean that sixth grade is sufficient as prerequisite to begin theological education.

5. *Economic extension.* The traditional method of theological education is very expensive, especially on the mission field. Extension programs can cut expenses drastically.

6. *Ecclesiastical extension.* The situation of a divorce between seminaries and local churches can be reversed by placing the 'seminary' in the local church and give people opportunity to relate to teachers and professors.[3]

What to Teach?

The traditional approach to theological education has been to train promising young men "for the ministry." The Bible speaks a lot about the spiritual gifts which the Spirit gives to individual members of the church. Some of these gifts are gifts of leadership or ministry, and in Ephesians 4:11 some of these gifts are mentioned: apostles, prophets, evangelists, pastors, and teachers.

The task of the lay-leadership-training program is to locate people to whom God has given the specialized gifts of ministry or leadership, and then train and assist them so that they will be able to use their gifts in the best possible way. Our teaching will therefore begin with the person and his gifts, not with a set curriculum.

If we base our leadership training on spiritual gifts, which have been tried and proven, we will find that the majority of our students are mature men with homes, families, jobs and community responsibilities. This is a description which does not too well fit the typical student whom most of us have been training through the years. It *does* fit 1 Timothy 3:1-7.[4]

The objects of lay-leadership-training are men and women who, generally, are not being trained by present missionary and church programs.

THE CASSETTES IN LAY-LEADERSHIP-TRAINING

It is fully realized that some of the material in this chapter builds on very limited experience. The urgent need for effective leadership training of leaders in the local churches has caused us to look for, and try, new media and methods. Usually new methods are not perfect from the beginning, so the new media, theories, and techniques require further study and research. The pressing need and the many requests for information are the reason for writing on the subject at this time. It is very probable that there will be intensive refinements in the next few years which are brought about by further experience and research. Such a project is ambitious and will require faith and hard work.

The Cassette Bible School in Thailand

The planning for the Cassette Bible School began in the middle of 1970, about one year after the introduction of Bible teaching cassettes in Thailand. Representatives from various Christian groups met at Voice of Peace in early 1971 to discuss the plans and to decide on a tentative program. The first study groups were formed in early 1972 so, at the time of this writing, less than two years have passed since the first cassettes were tested in the field.[5]

A brief overview of this work and the lessons learned

in Thailand will be given here. The rest of the chapter will be an elaboration of the various points.

1. The cassette forms the core of the study program.

2. The material on the cassette is a dialogue between a teacher and two "typical" students.

3. Supplementary material needed includes cassette player, Bible, texts, workbook or notebook or question sheets.

4. The complete program will use approximately 100 cassettes and will take 4-5 years to complete.

5. The scripts are programmed and culturally based, so they cannot be directly translated for use in other cultures.

6. Local pastors or missionaries act as supervisors for the study groups in their area.

7. As a prerequisite, the students must have 4 years of education or at least be able to read and write.

8. Preferably the students should study in groups of 3-5 people.

9. The group needs 5-8 hours to complete the work for each cassette and associated material.

10. The supervisor meets with the group about every 2 weeks.

Why Use Cassettes in Lay-Leadership-Training?

The main reasons that cassettes were considered for lay-leadership-training were that they gave good results in other phases of the teaching ministry, and they seemed to contain the needed ingredients to make extension teaching effective for this audience segment. Some advantages of the cassettes are:

1. Repetition. This is important in all learning, but it is even more important in view of the fact that most of the people with whom we deal have difficulty reading.

2. It is important to select media and tools the student can tune in to and feel relaxed and satisfied with. The cassette has proved to be such a tool.

3. Assisted by other material such as literature and practical projects, the material can be made relevant and alive to the student so that identification can be easily achieved.

4. By using cassettes, the teaching can be given any

time. There is no need to wait for a term to begin or for a teacher to be available. The schedule can fit in with anybody.

5. The cassette makes it possible to study almost anywhere, since only batteries are needed. No expensive, time-consuming travel is needed for the student.

6. The pace of the studies can be set by each group, or individual, as they decide.

7. A large number of students can study without the need for an increase in teaching staff. The local supervisors themselves do not need to prepare for teaching.

Good Teaching Principles Observed

How do people learn? There are different theories and methods of learning. The programmed instruction method is closely related to the stimulus-response theory and is behavioristic. This does not necessarily mean that the users accept a behavioristic view of man, but the empirical findings of scientific study of human behavior cannot be overlooked either.

Some people learn in groups by rote, others by individual study; some learn through storytelling, others by playing games.

If in a certain culture the teaching is by rote, then a person will learn less if he is introduced to another system of learning. Learning by rote is not necessarily inferior and may sometimes even be superior to other methods. In some cultures learning is done in the context of the family, not individually. For any new learning method to be accepted and effective, it must be compatible with the person's background and capabilities. A game might be a better exercise than an essay, and a dramatic story or legend might communicate more than a systematic lecture. In developing extension programs it is of the utmost importance that we are aware of these differences.

Dr. Ward observes some basic principles as to how people learn:

1. Learning proceeds best as the learner associates new information with information he already knows.

2. Learning (retention) depends on the use of newly acquired information very soon after it is acquired.

3. Learning depends on the perceived importance of information. The importance of information must not only be indicated or demonstrated for the learner, but he must also experience a situation in which he finds that the information relates to his own purposes and goals.

4. Learning (retention and accuracy) is increased when the learner is informed very promptly whether or not his use of new information is appropriate.[6]

The key words are "association," "use," "perceived importance," and "appropriate." Dr. Ward compares the learning experience to a split-rail fence. The cognitive learning and field experience are the two rails of the fence: the seminars and sharing times are the fence posts.

The Cassette Bible School closely follows these principles. The 'rails' are constructed by the course input and by the constant need to translate the learning into practical experience. The group study method and the regular meeting with the supervisor give ample "fence posts." Nevertheless, the fence will break down if important aspects of the instruction are overlooked by either the supervisor or the students.

RESEARCH NEEDED TO ESTABLISH BASIS FOR PROGRAMMING LEVEL AND CONTENT

The research outlined in chapter three will give quite a few clues to the teacher involved in a cassette lay-leadership-training program, but the findings mentioned there will not be enough. As a matter of fact, years of experience and search may be needed to find the ideal and truly effective program.

There are three areas that must be considered and researched before the program is even started. These areas concern the prospective student's: (1) educational background, (2) cultural environment, and (3) understanding of the Scriptures.

Educational Background of the Prospective Student

The questions that must be asked, and answered, will give the basis for the educational level of the extension program, but it must be remembered that an elementary education does not necessarily equate with an elementary understanding. What is the educational system under which the student studied? What method of teaching was used? How many years did he study? How long ago was that? What was he able to do when he finished school? What other learning experiences has the typical student of the extension program had? Does he read much? Does he read well? Does he enjoy reading? How does he generally receive news and information? Is the main source a newspaper, radio, television, or village 'opinion leaders'? The initial phase of a lay-leadership-training program may be directed towards the person with moderate intellectual development, and then later programs can be developed for higher or lower academic levels.

Cultural Environment of the Student

One of the great advantages of extension teaching is that it can be given within a person's own cultural environment. A thorough study of the culture is necessary. This is an exciting and rewarding part of the work. To take full advantage of the extention program potential, its strategies, approaches, and instruction material must all be based on the student's subculture.

For example, in the Orient it is a serious personal matter to "lose face." Many of our Western educational approaches, based on individualism and competition, would cause "loss of face" to many students and eventually break down the system. In group study, therefore, the group should be of an adequate size so that students can take turns reading aloud. In this way one or two won't have to read if it is too difficult for them. Our traditional approach may also require the sharing of personal views in a candid and direct way. A person from another culture may feel more at home if asked to communicate his views in a subtle way by telling a story or writing a drama. More honest responses may be obtained this way.

Understanding the Scriptures

Bible knowledge will vary from student to student, but in order to avoid being either too difficult or too easy, we have to find out how much we can assume about the typical student's Bible knowledge. We have to know his actual understanding of the Scriptures and how well he knows the Bible and its content. What is his understanding of Christian words, terms and concepts? What does he understand by such terms as God, sin, and prayer? What does the church mean to him? We should also try to discover his 'misunderstandings.' What areas does he have difficulty understanding?

Profile of the Student

The data obtained by research will enable us to establish a profile of the typical student. The profile of the typical Cassette Bible School student has been worked out. It should be remembered that we are referring to local church leaders, not the general church member. Some of the emerging points are:

He is a fairly new Christian with little opportunity to receive Bible teaching due to the fact that he is often in a place visited only periodically by a Bible teacher or missionary.

His religious background is the traditional Buddhist religion.

Years ago he attended school for about four years, but until he had the desire to read the Bible, he has not read very much at all.

He is a family man whose time is principally taken up with earning a living.

Economically, it is not feasible for him to take time off for formal Bible school training. Even if adequate finances were provided, he would have great difficulty fitting into a Bible school situation where fellow students would be mainly young people.

He has an earnest desire to study the Bible, not only for personal benefit, but in order that he may be able to pass this knowledge on to his relatives and friends.

He is mature in his outlook and confirmed in his vision to serve the Lord in the local church.

He is often called upon to minister to fellow Christians, as they have no pastor.

Apart from these general points, there is also specific information on education, culture, and understanding of Scripture.

The two students taking part in the dialogue on the cassette play the roles according to the typical student profile. This helps the students following the course at home to identify with them.[7]

PREPARING PROGRAM AND COURSE OBJECTIVES

No course should be included purely on the basis that everybody else teaches that course in a Bible school. In a person-centered program, the question is first asked, What does the student need to be able to perform his duties in the church?

Writing the Objectives

Stating objectives is, in a way, writing the exam questions before the course is made. Course content is needed to reach the objectives. It is important to be specific when writing objectives so that these objectives can be of real help. Objectives written in precise and technical language can tell the teacher if he has achieved the goals of his teaching, and it will show the student what is expected of him and what the course will teach him.

It is important to use precise words when stating objectives, so that it will be possible to measure the results of the program. Words like "to know," "to understand," "to appreciate," "to believe," and "to have faith in" are too ambiguous to be measurable. It is much better to use such terms as "to write," "to identify," "to list," and "to compare."[8]

It is important that our objectives are measurable. They should be stated in behavioral, or performance, terms that describe what a student will do in a certain circumstance, or as a result of a certain stimuli. Some examples are: "Given a list of 6 . . . the student will be able to . . . ." "When asked to . . . he will perform in such a way that . . . ." "When presented with this list of 20 questions, he will be able to answer at least 17 correctly."

It might seem difficult to be specific if the objective is to teach inductive Bible study, yet it can be done. By knowing the person's profile and having stated the specific objectives, the writing of the course content becomes a straightforward task which will be greatly rewarded when the objectives are achieved.

Curriculum

The basic questions to ask concerning curriculum are, What do you want to train the leader to do? What does he need to know to be able to do it? There is also the need of the church and its environment to take into consideration. Many courses given in theological institutions are being challenged as to purpose and relevancy. Some churches have unique needs, others want to place emphasis on certain aspects. The type of ministry in different situations require different courses. It is, therefore, not possible to establish a worldwide curriculum unless it consists of a lot of electives! Due to the experimental aspect of the Cassette Bible School, a tentative curriculum was decided on; but it may change if experience and need so indicate. The length of each course is indicated by the approximate number of cassettes. The tentative curriculum looks like this,

Elementary series on Christianity	6 cassettes
The Life of Christ	4 cassettes
Old Testament Survey	8 cassettes
New Testament Survey	6 cassettes
Basic Doctrines	8 cassettes
Psalms	4 cassettes
Isaiah-Jeremiah	4 cassettes
Minor Prophets	4 cassettes
Romans	4 cassettes
Revelation	3 cassettes
Relationship of O.T. and N.T. (Hebrews)	3 cassettes
The Church I and II	4 cassettes
Church History	2 cassettes
Buddhism	1 cassette
Spirit Worship	1 cassette
False Cults	1 cassette
Christian Ethics	2 cassettes
The Christian Family	2 cassettes
Stewardship	1 cassette
Prayer	1 cassette

Personal Witnessing	1 cassette
Evangelism	2 cassettes
Leading Meetings	1 cassette
Preparing a Sermon	2 cassettes
Public Speaking	1 cassette
Teaching Bible	2 cassettes
Children's Work	2 cassettes

Some of these courses are produced and others are being prepared. The production order does not follow the same order as listed above. A variety of subjects are needed from the beginning.

The students who started at the beginning of the project have more or less followed the production order of the courses; but as more and more courses are available, new students can select the ones most needed first. Everybody should begin with the elementary course in order to get the basic teaching given there, and also to be familiar with the study methods used.

PREPARING THE CASSETTES AND SUPPLEMENTARY MATERIAL

It is unrealistic to think that everything can be taught by cassettes. Not every course can be taught the same way either. Programmed texts and other self-instruction tools are great, but not for everything. The lay-leadership-training program, therefore, consists of more than the cassettes. There are workbooks, texts, exercises, projects, group discussions, counseling, and seminars. The cassettes play a major role, but the other parts are equally important. Together the various parts form one complete integrated course.[9]

If only cassettes were used, there would be so many needed that the program would be very expensive. Also, there are already many good books available with devotional and Bible study material. If people were reading these books, there would be no need for the cassettes, but they don't. The cassette then helps to accomplish several things. It helps people get into the reading by providing motivation, and it improves reading skill and comprehension of written material. The cassette also helps to improve a person's ability to find answers in written material and to write these answers down.

Preparation of Supplementary Material

The supplementary material will vary from course to course, but the following is usually needed: (1) Bible, (2) textbook, and (3) workbook.

Bible

Each student must have a Bible and, if possible, all students should use the same translation. Bible readings on the cassettes and Bible quotations in the text or workbooks should, if possible, also be from the same translation. Although this helps the students, no serious problems were experienced when two different translations were used.

Textbook

A book that will be used as a textbook in the Cassette Bible School must meet some important criteria. It must be well written, clear, and concise. The material must be well organized so that it can easily be broken up into neat sections. It should be easy to add paragraph numbers so that each paragraph can easily be identified by the student. Many of the available books—devotional, Bible studies—are not organized in this way. If a book is available and adaptable, then it may be possible to get the publisher to do a special printing, adding paragraph numbers. If no such book can be found, there is no other choice but to write one.

Five small, excellent books were used for the elementary (or introductory) course of the Cassette Bible School. One book (about 25 pages) was used for each cassette. A special printing was done and paragraph numbers added. This material was then used with question sheets. For the second course, a special workbook was printed as well.

Workbook

The workbook is for the student to work in, and is needed for both group and individual study. It may contain extra information, maps, sketches and diagrams, and questions for the student to answer.

The workbook may also be programmed. This makes the textbook, and other materials, much more effective.

If the workbook is not programmed, however, then the cassette "programs" every aspect of the course. A programmed workbook will largely take over the "programming" by guiding students through the course step by step.

If a programmed workbook is needed, the best procedure, first of all, is to select the textbook. Then prepare a rough copy of the workbook. Next the cassette will be made. This will enable the speaker to refer to exact places in both text and workbook, and it will be much easier to integrate all parts of the program. Figures 34 and 35 show two pages from a workbook prepared for the Cassette Bible School in Thailand.

Preparing the Script for the Cassettes

Though it is obvious that a script is needed for producing cassettes, the point needs to be emphasized. Some have tried to record live classroom sessions with students. Such a procedure cannot be accepted. It is not only too expensive, due to the number of cassettes needed, but it is also poor observance of communication principles.

The Basic Script Material

The basic script material may come from a variety of sources. The Cassette Bible School operates on an interdenominational basis, so teachers are recruited from various missions and churches. In this way people with a lot of experience in the country, who are authorities in their particular field, can contribute to the program. Each of these contributors has to be informed of the student profile and course objectives. If a textbook has been selected and workbook prepared, this has most likely been done in consultation with him.

How the basic script material is submitted to the Voice of Peace depends on the individual person. Some will do it on cassette, others in a written script. Those who are familiar with extension teaching are better able to prepare the basic script.

Programming Scripts

The basic script is edited by the Cassette Bible School staff and put into the form used on the cassettes. The

16 A B C	อ่าน ตอบ ตอบ ฟังเทป	OO OO	มาระโก 4.30–34 เมล็ดพืชในเรื่องนี้เป็นเมล็ดชนิดเล็กหรือโต พระเยซู ทรง อธิ บายความ หมาย ของคำ อุปมาให้ ใครฟัง เมล็ด มัสตารด
17	อ่าน ตอบ ฟังเทป	OO OO	มาระโก 4.35–41 เมื่อพระเยซูกับพวกสาวกข้ามทะเล มีเรือลำเดียว หรือหลายลำไปด้วยกัน พระเยซูทรงทำอะไร ในเวลาที่พายุเกิดขึ้น พระเยซูทรงห้ามพายุ
18	อ่าน ตอบ ตอบ ฟังเทป	OO OO	มาระโก 5.1–20 ทำไมชายที่มีผีสิงอยู่ เรียกชื่อตนเองว่ากอง ผีที่สิงอยู่ในชายคนนั้น อ้อนวอนขออะไรกับพระ เยซู เมื่อผีเข้าสิงอยู่ในฝูงสุกรนั้น อะไรเกิดขึ้นแก่ สุกร พระเยซู ทรงขับไล่ผีกอง ออกจากชายคน หนึ่ง
19	อ่าน ตอบ ฟังเทป	OO OO	มาระโก 5.21–34 ยาอีโร มีตำแหน่งเป็นอะไร ผู้หญิงในเรื่องนี้เป็นโรคมากี่ปี ผู้หญิงที่ถูกต้องชายฉลองของพระเยซู

Column 1: Paragraph number in textbook
Column 2: Instructions
Column 3: Space to check off work completed.
Column 4: Bible text to read, questions, heading for section on the cassette.

A: Read   B: Answer   C: Listen

Figure 34
Page from Thai Workbook

138

14. พวกทหารได้เตรียมอะไร   เพื่อให้พระเยซูดื่มก่อนที่จะถูกตรึงที่กางเขน

15. พระเยซูทรงทูลพระบิดาว่าอย่างไร   เมื่ออยู่บนไม้กางเขน

16. ถ้าไม่มีผู้ใครับโทษแทนเรา   พระเจ้าจะยกโทษให้คนบาปที่กลับใจได้หรือ
    ไม่

17. พระโลหิตของพระเยซูช่วยเราอย่างไรบ้าง

ข้ออภิปรายม้วนที่ 10

1. ปีลาตพยายามทำดีหรือไม่ เขาได้ทำถูกต้องหรือไม่ เพราะเหตุใด

2. บางคนออกความเห็นว่า ความเห็นของเปโตรที่ได้ปฏิเสธพระเยซู   ร้าย
   กว่าความผิดของยูดาที่ได้ทรยศต่อพระองค์ ท่านคิดอย่างไร โดยเหตุผล
   อะไร

3. ศีลมหาสนิทมีความสำคัญแก่เราแต่ละคน และแก่คริสตจักรของเราอย่าง
   ไรบ้าง

4. ในแคเสททีม้วนนี้ เปโตรแสดงความกล้าหาญอย่างไรบ้าง เขาแสดงความ
   ไม่กล้าอะไรบ้าง

Upper half: Questions for the individual to answer
Lower half: Discussion questions for the group.

Figure 35
Page from Thai Workbook

139

cassette consists of a dialogue between a teacher and two students, one man and one woman. These two students take the role of the typical student "studying" the course material used on the cassette. They ask questions of the teacher, and he asks them questions. The answers given by the students on the cassette are answers a typical student would give. If the typical student would give the wrong answer, then the student on the cassette gives the wrong answer and the teacher corrects him. In this way, good identification is achieved. Often the students following the course are asked to stop the cassette player to read a passage from the Bible, to do some kind of exercise, or to discuss a subject among themselves so they can see how it applies to their situation.

The programmed script is based on the basic script. The methods used are very similar to those used in programmed instruction, so the reader is advised to consult some of the books that already exist on that subject.

The dialogue on the cassette does not have to be all speaking, a chorus or hymn can also be used now and then. Sometimes a story or game may be used to illustrate a point.

As already mentioned, the script for the cassette must be thoroughly integrated with associated material, but it must also be a self-contained unit. It is expected that, after the group work, the cassette will be played again several times. Each time it should recap the major points for the student, making it possible for him to recollect the supplementary material. There will often be those listening who are not following the course, due to illiteracy or some other reason. A self-contained cassette will teach them something as well.

Figure 36 illustrates how a script may be written. All instructions are written in capital letters. The script is a page from a translation of the Thai script for the sixth cassette in the Elementary Course. The subject is "The responsibilities of the Christian."

The Recording

The techniques of recording will be discussed in the next chapter, but there are a few technical hints that should be given at this point.

Selecting the right voices is important. The one taking

| (TEACHER) | important in this section. Then write your thoughts down in your notebook. So now you may turn off the player and read chapter one in the textbook. |

SOUND OF BELL (FLUTE)

TEACHER	Have you finished reading? What do you then think is the most important thing in this chapter?
STUDENT 2 (WOMAN)	I think the most important thing in this chapter is that the Lord has done so much for us that we should show our love for Him by obeying His Word.
STUDENT 1	Yes, I also think that this is most important. When I read the Bible verse on page 8, I also felt that this verse is very important.
STUDENT 2	What verse was it?
TEACHER	Would you just read this verse for us, Sawaeng?
STUDENT 1	"Whether, then you eat or drink or whatever you do, do all to the glory of God."
TEACHER	Thank you, Sawaeng. I want you to memorize this verse today, because it is very important and is in a way the center of our obedience and Christian life. You can write this verse as the most important thing in this section, if you like, but also keep your own ideas.
	Now take your notebooks and open up on a new page. On the first line write this heading The Responsibilities of the Christian (REPEAT).

Figure 36
Translated Page from Script for a Cassette

the part of the teacher does not need to be the person who submitted the basic script. Generally it is better if he is not the voice on the cassette. The teacher must not only have an authoritative voice, but he also must be able to speak in a sharing way, as though he were speaking in the living room. The student parts probably will be recorded by the studio staff. They should sound authentic—like real students. The parts must be acted so they sound like real questions and answers—not like someone reading the script. The answers should be typical of a student.

Always remember that the students are studying at home in a small group. The background sound should place the speakers in their house, instead of in a church or auditorium. A right sound can make a big difference to the course.

The person will also need a few seconds to turn the cassette player off and on. A bell signal—or maybe a 2-second long note from an organ or flute—on the cassette may be used to indicate that the cassette should be stopped. It may take a few seconds before he gets the player turned off, so after the signal, wait a few seconds before continuing the dialogue. If the first sentence after the stop is of secondary importance it would also help, since the continuity would not be broken if the player should be stopped a second late.

PRETESTING THE CASSETTE

The cassettes, like all other material, must be pretested before final production. Even if the script material has been pretested, the first recording of a cassette should not be expected to be the final. In Thailand the first cassettes were recorded several times, tested, changed, and re-recorded. Only after satisfying test results should the final production be made. Five steps are suggested for the pretesting: (1) self-critique, (2) staff-critique, (3) testing with one student, (4) group testing, (5) field testing.

After any of these steps it may become apparent that revision is needed. When revisions have been completed and a product goes through the first four steps satisfactorily, the actual field testing can be started.

Self-critique

It is not enough to be hard on yourself when writing and producing. Listen critically to the production and try to put yourself in the place of the intended students. You will probably discover that there are several things you are not satisfied with. Maybe the natural flow of the dialogue needs improvements.

Staff-critique

One person working alone can rarely do as good a job as he can if colleagues are helping. This is especially true in the evaluation of programmed cassettes. There is a limit to what such testing can do, for it cannot exactly predict the reaction of the target student; however, it can point out problem areas. Most of all, colleagues can ask questions that need to be raised.

The actual testing of material with colleagues may take various forms. The whole staff may listen at one time, or perhaps just a small panel that reviews each new production. The group or panel may be together in one room, or scattered across the country, receiving the test copy by mail. On the mission field the panel must include at least one national worker.

Testing with one Student

The next step in the testing process should be with one of the students for whom the course in intended. The aim is to uncover any inadequacies and difficulties in the course. Before beginning the testing, the purpose of the testing should be explained to the student. He should be encouraged to make any corrections or suggestions that come to his mind. He will then receive the same introduction to the course as future students will receive.

The testing, by a student trying to follow the course, should be carried out by the writer/producer of the material. He should not help the student unless it is obvious that further progress cannot be achieved without help. He should encourage the student, and also listen very carefully to see how the student progresses through the course—what is easy? what is difficult? He should also watch for any outward signs that may give clues as to how the student understands the material. It would be a great advantage if you could encourage the student to think aloud.

Group Testing

The pretesting should point out major difficulties, but the material still has to be tested with a group to see how it will do under the real conditions. One of the study groups that is following the program can be used for this purpose. They should be informed that it is a test of the course, but apart from that they should be instructed to work through the material as they would do normally. The writer/producer should closely observe the group as they work with the material. He should not step in to help or correct any conclusions that they may reach. It is the program, not the student, that is being tested. If the student needs help, that is the same as pointing out a deficiency in the program. All through the session(s) the writer should take careful notes of his observations, If he can record the whole session, it may help him later. If the pretesting proceeds satisfactorily and no noticeable problems exist, then the program is ready for real testing in the field.

Field Testing

It should never be expected that a course is perfect when it is finally released for use. Most courses will need some changes due to inadequacies that show up when the program is run under the direction of local supervisors. Before rushing into printing the materials that go along with the course, the program should be tested with a few of the groups that are studying. This will be done without the presence of the supervisor or the writer/producer. After this testing period, which may last a few weeks, consultation should be conducted with both the supervisor and the students in order to get their reaction to the course. This also may call for a few changes. The course should now be ready for general distribution. A revised edition may be needed after a few months or years of use.

THE ACTUAL USE OF THE CASSETTE LAY-LEADERSHIP-TRAINING PROGRAM

The actual field work of an effective lay-leadership-training program by cassette involves several steps. In order to keep the program going smoothly, each of these steps must be carefully followed.

Meet with the Supervisor to Teach and Train Him

Supervisors are responsible for guiding the groups so

that students get the most out of the course: therefore they must be responsible, qualified people. In order to perform their duties, they need clear instructions as to how the supervision should be done.

Training the supervisor is explained in the chapter on personnel and training. Meeting with the supervisor involves selling not only the method to him, but also the importance of observing all the steps involved so that his own theories will not substitute the proven principles of the program. The training should make him feel comfortable with the program, and if possible it should involve field observation. In a widely scattered work, it may be necessary to prepare a special instruction book for the supervisors.

The supervisor should receive specific instructions that he may need for each course. Course objectives will be clearly outlined for him, and he will be told which points he should especially be careful about in the group session. Answers to the questions in the workbook should be provided to help him in correcting the student workbooks. After each course the student will be required to take an exam or complete a certain project. Since this will be under the direction of the supervisor, it would be helpful for him to know these questions beforehand.

Explaining the Study Principles and Methods to Students

For almost all of the students, the use of extension material by cassette will be new. It will demand the ability to change in his study habits, ways of learning, and the expectations that he has concerning the study. It is very important that a smooth beginning is achieved, so that he will get well into the course and enjoy the benefits before giving up in frustration. There should be a first session with the students, where the local supervisor will be assisted by the writer/producer or someone from the production staff. During that meeting the need for training is further explained. It is shown how the new method can meet these needs. The method is then carefully explained, and the students should try out a simple demonstration course.

An instruction cassette can be used to introduce the students to the voices on the cassettes. Such an instruction cassette can give some examples of "real" cassettes, and it can explain such sounds as a bell or flute that might be used to indicate when the cassette should be stopped. It can also give hints as to how they best can study individually and how to work in the group. It will also explain the importance of the meetings with the supervisor. The instruction cassette may also include a testimony or short devotion, challenging them to dedicate themselves to the study.

Supervision of the Group

The supervisor will meet with the group every two weeks. This meeting is very important in the total course context. The supervisor is the resource person for the group. He is their helper, instructor, counsellor, and advisor. He should also be able to assist with library facilities so that students who want and need more material can borrow books on the subject they are studying.

The place of meeting can be almost anywhere, but it should preferably be where students usually meet together and study. This can be the home of one of the students, or the supervisor's home—though this is not likely. In many places it will be in the local church building. The place should have some teaching facilities, such as a small blackboard. The time of the meeting can be any time it is convenient for the students and supervisor to get together. The best time is the time the students regularly meet, but this may not always work out if the supervisor has several groups under his supervision. A great deal of flexibility is possible at this point, but once the best time is decided, the schedule should be kept very regularly.

When the supervisor meets with the group, they have a short devotion together. Then the work done since last meeting is reviewed, and the new material is presented. This is further explained below.

If possible, the supervisor should give plenty of time to this meeting. If the meetings are frequent and he meets with the students in between, it is not too important to spend a long time with the group; but if there are 3 or 4 weeks between the meetings and they don't meet in between, the supervisor should be able to stay for longer time—maybe even overnight so he can counsel and help in assignments and projects.

146

Work in the Group

Students are advised to study in groups of 3 to 5, but this is not always possible. One man may have to study by himself in one village, while in another village there are too many students in the group.

Small group study affords many practical and rewarding benefits. Some of these are:

1. The same equipment—cassettes, players, batteries—is needed for a group as for one person.

2. Less proficient readers learn reading skill through following along with the group reading.

3. Discussion of study questions develops comprehension, skill, and ability to express one's opinions.

4. The group members learn to listen to each other.

The group will have a leader who will be responsible for starting and stopping the cassette player as directed. The function of the group leader is critical to the outcome of the studies, so the following points should be kept in mind when selecting him.

1. Any student in the group who is literate, dependable, and enthusiastic about studying may be a group leader.

2. He does not necessarily need to be much farther advanced in Bible knowledge than the others, but he must take the initiative.

3. His main responsibilities should be:

a. To handle the machine—starting and stopping according to instructions.

b. To direct the reading, making sure that the group works together smoothly.

c. To keep the lesson moving along as directed in cassette and workbook, thus assuring that listening, reading, and study-questions follow in proper order.

The group will decide on when and where to meet. There is no time limit, and they may meet any time of the day. It is expected that the first time they work through the material on one cassette, with associated material, it will take 3 to 4 hours, including the time spent reading, memorizing, writing, discussing, etc. They may go through the material a second time, but that will be much quicker. Altogether up to 8 or 10 hours may be needed. Generally speaking if they meet two or three nights a week, it should be enough. The supervisor will meet them one of these times every second week. One group was so enthusiastic

Cassette Bible school study group

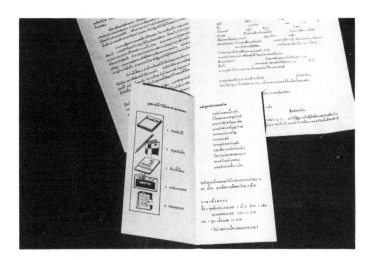

Cassette Bible school instruction material

Supplementary material for the cassette Bible school

149

Studying the Bible by cassette

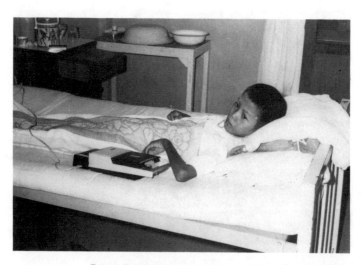

Evangelistic cassettes used in a hospital

Listening to a sermon on cassettes

Witnessing with a cassette

Recording the master tape

Voice of Peace studios

in the beginning that they began around 8 p.m. and continued to 2 a.m., but such enthusiasm usually wears off!

The group will follow the instruction on the cassette. When they are told to stop the cassette and read a Bible passage, for example, then they do that. One of the group will read the passage aloud. After the students have gone through the cassette once and followed all the instructions, they may find it best to do it once more together. Apart from that, the cassette should be made available for the individual members of the group to listen at home a few times. It will be most enriching if they also read the text, but the cassette is made so that, after the initial study, they will not have to turn the player off to read each passage. The material on the cassette is a continuous unit in itself. Of course, he can stop and read all the passages if he wants to.

The instructions will call for the students to discuss several questions together. This is aimed at making the material relevant to their own church situation and to their own lives. The advantage of a group is that they can help each other to get the right answers, and also encourage each other in the work.

Mistakes Done by the Group Leader

It cannot be assumed that the average person will automatically perform his functions correctly without careful instruction and observation in the beginning stages by the supervisor. Group leaders have made the following mistakes and they can seriously spoil the whole learning process.

1. He departs from the study pattern of listening and reading in regular sequence.

2. He decides to stop at frequent intervals to discuss the material. The listening and reading portions are closely related and should not be interspersed with discussion that may distract. Discussion should come during question period.

3. He doesn't see to it that books are laid aside when the tape is being played. Some students are inclined to continue reading when they should be listening. This must not be allowed.

4. He is the fluent reader in the group and does not set a reading pace that is comfortable for the slow readers.

5. He fails to encourage full participation in answering the study questions, or he simply gives the answers himself.

6. He lets the group try to answer question sheet at the same time as listening or reading are in progress. Special effort must be made to instill the habit of concentrating on the specific activity that is called for.

7. He neglects to shut off the tape when interruptions occur, such as when visitors arrive, or when other distractions draw the attention away from the lesson.

Personal Study

Apart from the group work, there is work for the individual student. Most of this is in the form of questions in the question sheet, workbook, or semi-programmed text. Each student should preferably answer these questions by himself. There may also be some scripture verses to memorize.

Each student should continually have assignments or projects. Since most of them already will be involved in church work, they should be encouraged to try out the material learned in their routine tasks. If they preach on Sundays, then they should be encouraged to make a sermon based on the material being studied, or they may teach it to a Sunday school class. The important thing is that the material learned will be put into focus immediately by using it in church. The learning experience is greatly enhanced by such a procedure.

Meeting with the Supervisor for Evaluation and Counseling

The question sheets filled out by the students may form the initial focusing point for the meeting with the supervisor. He may call on one or all students to read their answers to a certain question. The answers are then evaluated together in the group. Help and advice is provided by the supervisor. Whenever relevant, an application of the text or material should also be attempted. If the students have any problems, they should be dealt with.

The assignments and practical work of the students in the church should also be evaluated, and advice given on new projects. If such questions can be taken up in the group discussion, it will profit the whole group.

Finally, the supervisor will give the students the next cassette and associated material. The supervisor will encourage the students to continue the course and study diligently. Some of them may be finding the course difficult due to academic or spiritual problems, or it may be too hard for them to work and study at the same time. The encouragement and guidance by the supervisor will help the students through such times.

Exams, Projects and Seminars

At the end of each course, which may be from 2 to 5 or 6 months of study, there should be an examination. This will be taken under the direction of the supervisor. The student should receive some kind of recognition for work done, and when he has successfully completed a certain number of courses, a certificate should be presented to him.

The type of exam may change from course to course. Some exams may be of the traditional types, but in other subjects a practical project may prove more helpful than a written exam.

If several groups are studying in one area, a retreat or seminar every 2-3 months could be an extra help to the students. It is not necessary that all have completed the same number of courses. The material taught in an area seminar will basically be devotional in nature. It may also have some specialized subjects or points that all can follow and learn from. But the fellowship they receive at such a seminar is the main experience that will encourage and bless them.

The aim of the Cassette Bible School has been to build a teaching program that is effective and suited for the position and environment of the local church leaders in Thailand. The program uses a variety of materials in a system of personal and group study together with evaluation and teaching sessions. The following quotation from "The Split Rail Fence" by Dr. Ward expresses some of the same purpose.

> If a student is to make a solid connection between cognitive input and his field experiences, he needs someone to talk to—preferably someone who is learning along with

156

him. Perhaps it isn't quite a matter of magic, but something exciting happens when learners get together to put into *words* how new information relates to their doing an effective job. If left to chance or individual initiative, new information may never result in appropriate changes in the professional practice, or worse yet, it will result in incorrect applications to practice. Misunderstandings in the cognitive realm can result in disasters in the realm of practice. The seminar, as an opportunity for reflecting, evaluating and hypothesizing, can reduce the gaps and the misapplications, resulting in more potent and responsible transfers from "theory" to "practice," and back again to better theory." [10]

CONTINUITY IN THE LAY-TRAINING PROGRAM

Any new educational program, especially if new and untried methods and means are used, is bound to run into some problems concerning continuity. There will be problems in keeping up production as well as in keeping the groups functioning over a long period of time. This is especially true in a society where stick-with-it-ness is not a strong point. The following three suggestions may help to overcome such problems.

Good Planning and Constant Research

Good planning will include clear objectives and good organization. The work is planned on the basis of research and should be constantly evaluated by research. This can be done by interviewing students, supervisors, and production staff whenever possible. It will mean constantly watching for possible problems so that they can be solved before eruption. After a period of time a good research program should be carried out to establish the effectiveness of the courses.[11]

Encouraging Students and Supervisors

Encouraging supervisors may be a difficult task but specific steps can be taken. For example there could be retreats or seminars for supervisors once a year. Here they can share experiences and be a tremendous help to the production staff. Regular visits to the various areas where the material is being used will help.

The students need to be encouraged by the supervisors and the regular area seminars. A school paper might be a good idea so that news, testimonies, etc., can be circulated regularly to all students. This should not only be news concerning the program, but also church news of general interest.

Establish a Good Financial Basis

A realistic approach to the financial side of the course at the very beginning will help to eliminate later questions. Before starting the course, students should know exactly what it will involve financially. The mission or church may help to provide funds for cassette players, which are somewhat expensive to buy. A system can then be set up by which they pay a small monthly amount. This will not only pay for the material used, but also it will pay for the cassette player in a couple of years. Some churches or missions may be able to subsidize the players, or even buy them and let the study groups borrow them for the studies, since the whole church will profit if the leaders are trained. It is strongly advised that each student pay at least a small amount each month for the study. This will make it more valuable to him, and it will encourage him to continue to get the most out of it.

CHAPTER 8

Production Facilities

The need for adequate technical facilities is usually the biggest hurdle that confronts missionaries involved in building a cassette ministry. These problems, which for some seem almost impossible, can be greatly reduced by good planning and effective cooperation. It is necessary that good facilities are available, but it is not necessary that everybody have such facilities. For churches in most Western countries, the question of production facilities is not a serious one; several professional Christian organizations specialize in the production of cassette material for other organizations, and some churches have established their own facilities.

There are several reasons why high quality production equipment is needed. First, good quality is a necessity if the productions are to be used widely by various missions and churches. Only high quality equipment is able to produce good quality! Also adequate professional equipment saves time. To produce a master tape for cassettes is often as complicated as the production of dramatic radio programs—and to do that full control-room facilities must be available.

Another factor is economy. Professional equipment is expensive to purchase, but in the long run it will be cheaper, for it will last longer, be more reliable, and there will be fewer breakdowns, saving valuable time.

OVERVIEW OF EQUIPMENT
AND FACILITIES NEEDED

For cassette production, there are three different types of facilities: (1) basic field recording facilities, (2) studio and control room facilities for production and editing, and (3) high-speed cassette duplicating facilities. These classifications serve as a good guideline but, while some cassette ministries will have all three types of facilities, others will have only one or two. Technical facilities can also be classified according to the equipment involved: field recording equipment, studio, production equipment, cassette copying equipment, and service facilities.

The basic field recording facilities will include at least one high quality tape recorder and one microphone. If a small mixer and one or two additional microphones and stands are available, the recording possibilities will be multiplied; and if a small, simple studio can be built, the recording quality and procedure can be greatly improved.

Tapes recorded in the 'field' would be sent to the studio for editing and the production of master tapes. The equipment available there should include a recording studio and an accompanying control room with at least three tape recorders, mixer, and turntable. Some kind of music library will also be available.

The cassette duplicating facilities will be able to make cassette copies from the master tape on high-speed equipment.

Every mission field that enters the cassette ministry must have basic recording facilities, so that cassettes and the cassette players can be serviced in the country.

Strategically placed cassette duplicating facilities will be able to serve many churches and missions effectively and economically. The same is true for studio and control room facilities, but these facilities are already available in most countries in the form of radio production studios.

RECORDING EQUIPMENT

Several pieces of equipment are needed to produce the master tape. They include tape recorders, microphones, mixer, studio, tapes and a turntable. Each piece of equipment will be explained separately, then shown how they can be used together in productions. In all cassette productions a master tape is made first, and then the cassettes are duplicated from that tape. The master tape may be a high quality cassette but, as it is very difficult to edit a cassette, it is suggested that ordinary open-reel master tapes are made. If the high-speed duplicating equipment only copies from cassettes, then a duplicate of the open-reel master can be made on a high quality cassette recorder.

Recording Studio

A recording studio is a room that is soundproof and acoustically treated so that a good and natural sound can be picked up by the microphone. It is important that the studio is not too 'live,' giving an echo effect, or too 'dead,' absorbing the sound. It is also important that all sound frequencies can be picked up.

The purpose of this section is not to explain how a professional studio is made, for those establishing a studio will either have the know-how or they will study the subject in detail in technical books. This section will only try to describe how a studio can be made in an existing room, and then indicate ways recordings can be made under difficult conditions.

A missionary may improve his recordings greatly by making a small recording studio. A room in the house can be acoustically treated and used as a studio, but there are four things to take into consideration. (1) size, (2) isolation, (3) acoustics, and (4) air.

Size

The ratios—height, width, length—of a studio determine to a great extent the quality of the recordings. This is especially important for music. There is some leeway, but the average studio should have dimension ratios as follows: height—1.00, width—1.60, length—2.50. This means that if the height of the room is 10' then the width should be 16' and the length 25'.

Isolation

By selecting a room in a quiet house and area, many of the problems will be resolved. Studio isolation is usually obtained by installing double walls and ceiling, then filling the space between the walls with sound-absorbing material such as rockwool. The window to the control room needs to have double heavy glass.

Acoustics

The sound in the studio has to be diffused in such a way that it will not reverberate or cause echo. Two walls, therefore, cannot be exactly parallel, for this will cause the sound to reverberate. Panels should be used to break up some of the wall surface. Sizes and shapes of panelling can be varied, but they must cover at least 50% of the wall space. The floor must be flat—covered by rugs or mats—and the ceiling needs panels, too. Figure 37 gives some suggestions for panel forms.

Figure 37
Panels for Acoustical Treatment of Studio

The empty spaces inside the panels should be partly filled with rockwool or soft insulation. Heavy draperies or bamboo mats on the studio walls can also help with the acoustics.

Air

The studio will be completely closed by the sound-proofing material, so air has to enter somewhere without letting in noise. The only satisfactory solution in the tropics is air-conditioning. But since air-conditioners make noise, they have to be installed well away from the studio. Then the cold air is led through a long duct to the studio, and another duct returns air to the air-conditioner. Ducts need to be well insulated with fiberglass. A couple of bends in the duct will further reduce noise level.

Living Room Studio

It may not always be feasible to make a studio, so how can a living room be used for recording? Here are some suggestions.

1. Close all windows and outside doors to keep noise and draft out.

2. Open doors to another room in order to break the room up acoustically.

3. Pull curtains for the windows and hang heavy coats or blankets on walls and over chairs to absorb sound.

4. Experiment to find the best microphone position. Maybe a corner will be best, with the microphone facing the corner.

5. Use directional microphones that pick up sound from one direction only.

6. Record with microphone close to the performer.

7. If several people are involved use 2 or 3 microphones close up instead of one microphone for all.

Microphones

Microphones are available in all kinds of quality, shapes, and prices. A microphone is like a single ear, so it will pick up the same sound as one would hear with one ear just in front of the speaker. The principle function of a microphone is to pick up these sound vibrations and and convert them into electrical energy or impulses.

Microphones differ in the way they are made but, for our present purposes, only two kinds of microphones need to be considered: Dynamic microphones and condenser microphones.

Dynamic Microphones

These are cheaper than condenser microphones and, for most mission field work, they will be the preferred microphone to use. Dynamic microphones are quite rugged, versatile, and they come in a wide quality range. The better ones can produce high quality work. Dynamic microphones used in recording work should have a frequency response range from at least 40 to 13,000 Hz.

Condenser Micropohones

These are quite expensive, but they also have the best fidelity. The frequency response is excellent and the output level is good and even. If recordings are done in a studio, condenser microphones should be considered. For choir recordings, or other music recordings, the condenser microphone will give much better results. One of the problems in using a condenser microphone outside a studio—or church—has been that it needs a power supply unit to operate the small pre-amplifier which is built into the microphone, but some newer types of condenser microphones only need a single AA cell to operate the pre-amplifier. Condenser microphones are used widely in broadcasting and professional recordings.

Shapes of Microphones

The different shapes of microphones are usually due to the intended use. Microphones are, therefore, often classified according to how they are used. "There are nine types of television microphones: (1) boom microphones, (2) hand microphones, (3) lavalier and lapel microphones, (4) desk microphones, (5) stand microphones, (6) hanging microphones, (7) concealed microphones, (8) wireless (FM) microphones, and (9) 'long-distance' microphones." [1]

In recording for cassettes, the shape of the microphone is usually irrevelant. Theoretically each of the above mentioned microphones could be either dynamic or condenser microphones.

Recording Patterns of Microphones

The recording pattern, or directional characteristic of a microphone is very important. There are three basic patterns: uni-directional (or cardioid), omni-directional, and bi-directional (or figure 8 pattern).

Omni-directional   Uni-directional   Bi-directional
                        (Cardioid)

Figure 38
Directional Characteristics of Microphones

The dynamic microphones usually have either uni- or omni-directional characteristics. The condenser microphones are usually either omni-directional, or they may have eight or more patterns that can be selected by a switch. This, of course, greatly facilitates recordings, as the best pattern can be selected and unwanted sounds are placed outside the 'recording pattern.'

Microphone Impedance

There is one further point that must be considered concerning microphones, and that is the impedance. There are 'high impedance' and 'low impedance' microphones, and the inputs to a mixer or tape recorder will be either high or low impedance. The impedance figure is given in ohm, e.g., 50 ohm or 25,000 ohm. The microphone must be matched to the input. Such matching can be achieved by a small transformer. A high impedance microphone cannot have a cable of more than 12-15 feet, or hum and other noises will be picked up. For longer cables low impedance should be used so, if the microphone has a high impedance output, a transformer must be inserted. The impedance should be matched as closely as possible. A high impedance cable has only one wire with a shield around it, and a low impedance cable has two wires with a shield around it.

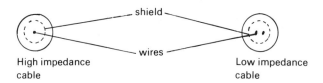

High impedance cable

Low impedance cable

Figure 39
Microphone Cables

Tape Recorders

The Principle of a Tape Recorder

A tape recorder contains both mechanical and electronic precision equipment and is somewhat more com-

165

plicated than other electronic equipment. To manufacture a tape recorder which will be able to operate perfectly during years of constant use is, therefore, not cheap. For recording studio purposes a high quality and constant dependability is needed and required.

The tape recorder receives the 'sound' from a microphone or other source in the form of electrical impulses. These impulses are amplified and then sent to the recording head which is a small precision electromagnet. When the transport mechanism pulls the tape past the recording head, the 'sound' is transferred to the tape as magnetic lines. In the playback mode, these magnetic fields on the tape are 'picked up' by the playback head which in turn sends electronic impulses to the amplifier. Finally, a loudspeaker transforms the signals into audible sound.

Heads and Tracks

Most tape recorders have three heads: erase head, record head, and playback head. The number of tracks that can be recorded depends on how the heads are made. There are full track, half track (or 2 track), and quarter track (or 4 track) heads. The full track uses all the tape in one recording, the half track is able to record 2 tracks on the same tape, and the quarter track puts 4 different tracks on the same tape. For mono recordings only 1 track is used, but stereo recordings require 2 tracks at the same time. For 2- or 4-track tape recorders, the tape is turned over to record on the other track(s).

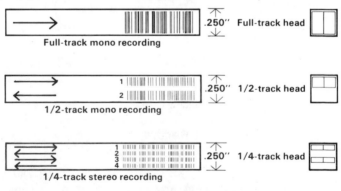

Figure 40
Open-reel Tape

166

The cassette recorders are a little different. The tape is narrow when compared with an open-reel tape. The heads of a cassette recorder are made in such a way that complete compatibility is obtained between mono and stereo.

Figure 41
Cassette Tape

For professional recording a full-track machine is usually used. If a 2-track recorder is used, then only track 1 is recorded. Due to the use of high-speed cassette recorders that copy both tracks at the same time, cassette master tapes will need to be 2-track recordings.

Speed

The speeds are standardized at 15", 7 1/2", 3 3/4", 1 7/8" or 15/16" per second. For master recordings and library tapes, the highest speed is advised. In the Christian ministry, we rarely see speed higher then 7 1/2" used, but that is sufficient. The final master tape for a cassette duplicator may have to be recorded at speed 3 3/4". The cassette recorders and cassette players run at the slow speed of 1 7/8".

Tape

Types of Tape

The quality of tapes have constantly been improved, and some of the newer products on the market are of extremely high quality. Good tapes are lubricated so they pass smoothly over the heads of the tape recorder. They are stronger and more difficult to ruin. Some new tapes are pre-stretched (tensilized) to make them more resistant to stretch. The frequency ranges in some cases are from 20 to beyond 30.000 Hz.

Recording tape consists of a 'tape-base' that is coated

with ultrafine magnetic iron oxide particles. Through the years different types of tape-base have been used, but now most are either acetate, polyvinyl chloride (PVC), or polyester. Acetate is cheaper and breaks more easily. Some good acetate tapes are on the market, but polyester or PVC is recommended for master tapes. Only polyester or PVC is acceptable for cassettes.

Tape Thickness and Size

The thickness of a tape varies. Standard tape is 1 1/2 mil, long play 1 mil, and double play 1/2 mil. The thinner the tape is the more of it can be put on a reel but, at the same time, the tape will be more delicate and difficult to work with.

Reel sizes are also standardized, and the most commonly used sizes are 7" and 5". A 1200' standard play tape will fit a 7" reel, and at a speed of 7 1/2" it will give 30 minutes of playing time on each track. On the tape chart the playing time for each track (one side) is given.

Type	Reel size	Length	Playing time each track		
			7 1/2"	3 3/4"	1 7/8"
Standard play	5"	600'	15	30	60
	7"	1200'	30	60	120
Long play	5"	900'	23	45	90
	7"	1800'	45	90	180
Double play	5"	1200'	30	60	120
	7"	2400'	60	120	240
Triple play	5"	1800'	45	90	180
	7"	3600'	90	180	360

Figure 42
Tape Chart

Tape Use and Storage

It is strongly suggested that only good quality, low-noise brand-name tapes are used, and they should be either standard or long play. Even though some new tapes are not supposed to be influenced by temperature or humidity, it is advisable to observe the following simple rules.

Keep tapes clean.
Keep tapes stored in an air-conditioned room.
Keep tapes in neither too dry nor too humid places. (40%-60% humidity best).
Keep tapes in plastic bags.
Keep tapes in labeled boxes.

Sound Mixer

The 'mixing' of various sound sources will often be called for in recording and production. In the mixer, the sounds from different sources are combined. The volume of each individual source can be controlled so that the right blend will be achieved. The uses of a mixer are many. Several microphones may be needed in a recording, but the voices differ in strength. Speech may be needed over background music, or maybe taped portions need to be mixed with live recordings.

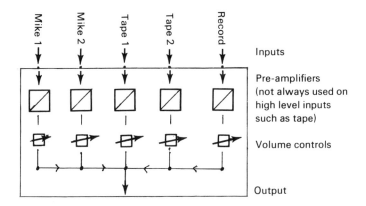

Figure 43
Principle of a Sound Mixer

169

A mixer will, therefore, have inputs for each microphone, tape recorder, and record player, as shown on figure 43. The output from the mixer then goes into the tape recorder.

Good mixers will improve or correct the sound signals coming in, and they may be able to add an echo or reverberation effect, which may sometimes be needed. The bigger mixers will also have a 'cue-system' that enables the control room operator to prepare the various parts before they are needed, while recording is in progress. A small basic 3 or 5 channel mixer for field recording is cheap, and it will facilitate the work. A good mixer will be as expensive as a tape recorder.

Putting the Equipment Together

Basic field recording facilities may be very modest. As far as equipment is concerned, a tape recorder or high quality cassette recorder together with a good microphone may be able to do the job. It is suggested, though, that the following equipment be considered minimal.

One high quality tape recorder
Three microphones (2 uni-directional, 1 omni directional)
Microphone stands
Small microphone mixer
Earphones
(Small studio)

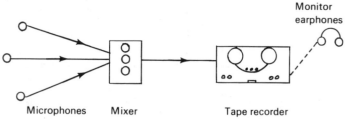

Microphones   Mixer   Tape recorder

Figure 44
Basic Recording Equipment

Full control room facilities needed for the production of the master tape are basically the same as in a radio studio. The following minimal equipment is needed.

3 tape recorders (or decks)
Sound mixer
Record player
Microphones
Monitor amplifier
(Studio)

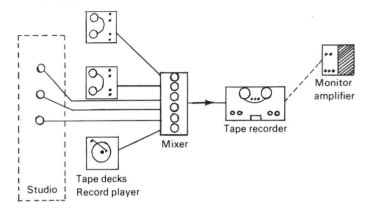

Figure 45
Full Control Room Facilities

Maintenance of Production Equipment

The magnetic recording heads form the very heart of a tape recorder, and they play a major role in determining the quality of the recording and playback. Servicing tape heads can easily be done by most people. Because of the importance of the tape heads, most of this section will discuss this subject.

Any recording ministry must be able to get their equipment repaired. Many books are available for the person who wants to study the subject more, but if a tape recorder (especially a professional machine) breaks down, a trained technician is needed to repair it. This section deals only with the daily care that will help reduce breakdowns and insure consistently high quality recordings.

Service Tools

To establish complete maintenance facilities, a wide variety of tools and testing instruments are needed, but for the 'non-professional-technician' the following tools are suggested:

Set of screwdrivers
Needle-nose pliers
Wire stripper and cutter

Set of allen wrenches
Small adjustable wrench
Soldering iron
Solder
Inspection mirror
Small maintenance brush
Oil
Multi-meter

Ethyl alcohol
Q-tips
Liquid or spray head cleaner
Cotton wool
Small (bamboo) sticks
Head demagnetizer
Cassette demagnetizer
Tape splicing block
Splicing tape
Alignment tape
Alignment cassette

Spare Parts

A few spare parts should always be on hand. If only one type of tape recorder is used, only one set of spares is needed; otherwise, each machine will need a set of spare parts. Here are some suggestions.

Fuses—at least a couple of each type used in the equipment.
Plugs—for all connections.
Cords—especially for microphones.
Drive belts—most recorders have a couple of drive belts.
Pressure roller—all tape recorders have one.
Pressure pad material and glue to secure it.
Set of tape heads—includes erase, record, and playback heads.
Tubes—a complete set for any equipment that uses tubes.

Daily Care

A few minutes of daily care is needed before the recording work begins. The morning clean-up! Basically, a clean machine will consistently give good performance, so always keep the recorder free from dust and dirt.

The daily care centers around the path of the tape.

172

Each part that the tape touches should be cleaned of dirt and iron oxide.

Use a brush to get dirt and dust away from places around reels.

Clean tape guides carefully. Use a little alcohol on cotton wool or Q-tips and polish them carefully.

Rub the pressure roller clean. Ethyl alcohol will not harm the rubber, but be careful with methyl alcohol as it may harden the rubber. A soft, wet cloth may also be used to clean the pressure roller.

Oxide on the capstan can be cleaned with cotton wool and alcohol.

Clean the tape heads so that they are absolutely clean. (See section on tape head maintenance later in this chapter.)

Clean the pressure pads, or change them if they are too dirty to clean. Improper adjustment of pressure pads will cause rapid, uneven wear of heads.

REGULAR MAINTENANCE

A more thorough maintenance check should be regularly carried out, preferably by a technician. Clean every part of the machine. Check drive belts and pulleys for any accumulated dirt. Check tape speed and adjust if necessary. Align and demagnetize tape heads. Most manuals supplied with the equipment and service tools tell how to do it. A technician should also check such things as bias, noise level, and equalization.

There are some 'outside' sources that may cause problems. Carefully check microphone cords and plugs. If wires are loose, broken, or poorly soldered, hum and other noises may be picked up. Another frequent difficulty is the power supply. In some places the voltage goes up and down, and the cycles (frequency) may fluctuate. The voltage can be stabilized by a 'constant voltage transformer.' If the frequency is erratic, the problem is much worse. Either another type of power supply is needed, or all tape recorders of a type with servo-control motors.

Maintenance of Tape Heads

As mentioned already, the tape heads are a very important part of the tape recorder. The condition of the tape heads not only influences frequency response and the general quality of the recording and playback; they may also ruin pre-recorded tapes. To avoid such problems careful maintenance of tape heads is needed.

THE TAPE HEADS

The recording and playback heads may appear identical. Some machines have one of each, others combine the two and use a single record/playback head. Separate recording and playback heads make it possible to monitor the recorded signal during recording. Apart from 'playback only' machines, all tape recorders have an erase head as well. The heads are placed as indicated on figure 46.

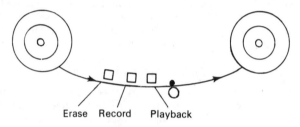

Erase   Record   Playback

Figure 46
Position of Tape Heads

The record and playback heads consist of a core wound with a coil of extremely fine wire. (The wire in the record head is a little more coarse than that used in the playback head.) The two pole tips of the core are exposed on the face of the head separately by a very fine gap ranging from 50 to 500 millionths of an inch in width. This gap extends the width of the head track and is oriented vertically at a right angle to the edge of the tape.

During the recording process, the tape is drawn across the face of the head. The audio signals (current) from the recording amplifier pass through the head coil, magnetizing the pole pieces and creating a magnetic field across the gap. This in turn generates a series of permanently magnetized lines which are impressed into the iron oxide of the tape.

The tape is 'prepared' to receive these lines by the bias signal which is mixed with the audio signal. The right

174

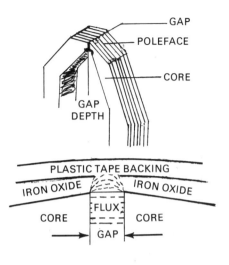

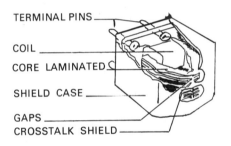

SECTIONAL VIEW OF STEREO RP HEAD

Figure 47

Tape Heads

Drawings by Nortronics, Minneapolis, Minn. Used by permission.

adjustment of this bias frequency is important.

During playback the process is reversed. The magnetic lines induce a voltage in the coil of the playback head in a true reproduction of the original recording.

SERVICE OF TAPE HEADS

Such delicate instruments can easily be damaged, so inspect the heads carefully and often. When the tape passes over the face of the head, some iron oxide may be left on the head. Tape heads should, therefore, be cleaned after a few hours of use. Various cleaning sprays are available, but usually cleaning is done best by using a Q-tip and ethyl alcohol. Carefully wipe off all dirt accumulated on the head. Don't press hard, and be careful not to scratch the head in any way. Be careful to use only wooden sticks.

The heads may occasionally become misaligned so that the gap in the head is not exactly vertical.

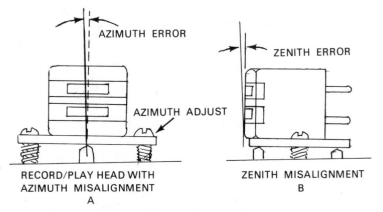

Figure 48
Misalignment of Tape Heads
Drawings by Nortronics, Minneapolis, Minn. Used by permission.

The best way to adjust alignment (azimuth error) is to use an alignment tape. Play this tape and adjust the screw on the playback head until maximum output is obtained. Then use a blank tape and record a constant, high tone. During this recording, monitor the output signal from the playback head and adjust the screw on the record head until maximum output is obtained.

A frequently overlooked, but important area of maintenance is head demagnetizing. As the recorded tape goes past the heads, they may become permanently magnetized, and when that happens they can partially erase valuable recordings. Demagnetizing can easily be done with one of the commercially available demagnetizers, but remember to turn the demagnetizer off or on at some distance from the heads. Also be sure demagnetizer pole tips are covered with tape or a similar soft covering to avoid scratching head faces.

Tape heads usually last for hundreds of hours of use, but they do wear down. Rough or sharp edges on the head will indicate wear. Also a visual inspection may reveal separation or widening of the gap. Whenever symptoms of headwear are heard, or felt, the head will need to be replaced.

PRODUCING THE MASTER TAPE

This work includes basically two phases: (1) actual recording, and (2) editing or producing the master tape.

Recording

So many factors are involved in making a good recording that the following few suggestions can only be given as guidelines. Studio recording is assumed, but only experimentation and critical listening will produce good recordings.

The Tape Recorder

Select the right speed, usually 7 1/2", and record only one track on each tape. Be sure to keep tape heads clean. All tapes should be erased before recording. Use only tapes of good quality and in good condition.

How Many Microphones?

If only one person is speaking, a single microphone is sufficient, but with a group or panel, it is preferable to use 2 or 3 microphones. In music recordings, separate microphones are needed for vocal and instrumental pick up. The general tendency is to use as few microphones as possible for classical music, but several microphones for modern types of music.

Types of Microphones to Use

Always use uni-directional microphones if possible. For an interview across the table, 2 uni-directional or 1 bi-directional microphone should be used rather than 1 omni-directional. Make sure that the microphone pattern picks up what you want, not the distracting noise. Uni-directional microphones can eliminate many distracting sounds, which the omni-directional microphone picks up.

Handling Microphones

If at all possible, a microphone should never be in the hand during recording; it should be placed on a stand or microphone boom. Every touch by the hand will be picked up as a loud noise. Even a microphone placed on a table may be touched by hands or scripts, so it is better to let it come in over the table on a boom.

Placement of Microphones

For speaking, the microphone should be about one foot from the speaker's mouth. If several people are involved, they can either be around one microphone or several microphones. Then there is always a problem with the differences in the loudness of individual voices. This can be corrected by either placing them at different distances from the microphone, or by using different microphones that can be controlled individually at the mixer.

The distance of a soloist will depend on both microphone and voice. If a singer can work close to the microphone, a clearer and more intimate sound will be recorded, but this requires experience. Working close to the microphone makes the distance critical, since sound level increases and decreases drastically by movement. The soloist may have to move in and out slightly during various parts of the recording.

Experimentation

It is too involved to explain details of microphone placement and techniques. The best advice is to experiment with your equipment, studio, and voices. Several attempts may be needed before satisfactory sound is picked up.

Monitoring

All recordings must be monitored. If no control room is available, earphones should be used during recording. In the control room, a monitor amplifier and loudspeaker is preferred. The level of each microphone is adjusted first, and then all are monitored together. The final judge is always your ears!

Don't Edit While Recording

Tape editing should be kept in mind during recordings, but it is too complicated to edit during the actual recording. Simply put everything on the tape, then clearly label the box with information about content, performers, and time.

Recording in the Open-Air or Under Poor Conditions

The following suggestions will help to improve recording under poor conditions.

Study recording procedures and techniques and follow the ideal as close as possible.

Place the speaker in front of a solid background that will cut out noises from behind.

Select as quiet a spot as possible.

Use a highly uni-directional microphone.

Operate the microphone as close to the performer as possible.

Select a time when the external noises are limited.

Record in a car with closed windows.

Use windshield over microphone to cut out noises from the wind.

The Master Tape

Objectives and Standard

A master tape is the finished production from which cassette copies are made. It is strongly suggested that they all be made according to the standards needed for high-speed duplication. Even if such facilities are not available at the moment, they may become available later on, so make all master tapes to that standard.

The length of the cassettes will govern the length of the master tape. Usually C60 cassettes are used, playing 30 minutes on each side. This means that the master tape contains two 30 minute programs. Some C60 cassettes are a few minutes longer, but others play exactly 30 minutes, so the master tape has to be exactly 2 x 30 minutes. The length of the tape needed for master tape also depends on the desired speed. Due to the high-speed duplication speeds, a 3 3/4" speed is often used. For this purpose, select a 5" 600' tape for the master tape. If the master tape is going to be copied onto a master cassette for the duplicator, it may be better to use 7 1/2" speed for the production, in which case a 7" 1200' tape is needed.

The high-speed duplicator will copy both tracks at the same time, so the two programs have to begin and end at the same spot on the master tape, as illustrated on figure 49.

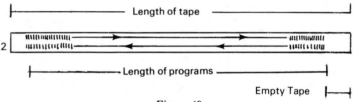

Figure 49
Position of Programs on Master Tape

When the program on track one is exactly 30 minutes long, turn the tape over and begin production on track two at exactly that point.

Production

First, collect all the tapes, records, and live talent that may be needed for the program. A script or rundown sheet must of course be supplied. With the help of the mixer, all program segments will be recorded, or copied, onto the master tape. If editing is necessary, just stop the recorder and leave the undesired parts out.

Script or Rundown Sheet

The rundown sheet for the cassette program to be pro-

180

duced may simply state the individual items and times.

1.	Instrumental Music: Tape No. 4 beginning	1.00 min.
2.	Interview: Mr. Smith/Mr. Taylor. Tape No. 19	4.00 min.
3.	Hymn: I Love to Tell the Story.	
	Record No. 14, side 1/3	2.30 min.
4.	Message by Rev. Lewis	5.00 min.
	Etc. etc.	
	Total	30.00 min.

If instrumental music is used at the end of a program, it gives some leeway in time for the music to be faded out exactly on time. At the end of each program, on each side of the tape, there should be a clear tone or announcement to tell the listener that it is time to turn the cassette over. The other side begins exactly there, even though there might still be a couple of minutes of empty tape.

Tape Splicing

Usually it is enough to splice tapes that are broken. Editing is easier done by simple dubbing, not by cutting.

The purpose of splicing is to put a broken tape together so well that the splice will not be noticed during playback. Careful and exact splicing should be mastered by all who work with tapes. There are a number of tools available, but the basic ones are the splicing block, a razorblade, and splicing tape. The steps of splicing are: (1) Cut the tape ends at approximately a 45^0 angle. Both ends are cut at the same time. (2) Join the tape ends exactly with no gap between and no overlap. (3) Place splicing tape on the back side of the tape (usually the shiny side), at least 1/4" on each side of the splice. No tape goes on the coated side, and use only real splicing tape that is specifically made for that purpose. (4) Trim any splicing tape that sticks out over the edges of the recording tape. (5) Rub the splice with the back of your fingernail to make sure there is a solid grip, but don't handle the tape ends more than necessary.

CASSETTES AND DUPLICATION

It is assumed that several, perhaps hundreds, of copies will be needed of each "program," so duplication of cassettes has to be done. High-speed duplication is desired, but not a necessity.

Duplicating Systems

Cassettes can be duplicated simply by connecting two cassette recorders, or a cassette recorder and a tape recorder. Technical advice is suggested if several cassette recorders are to be connected parallel, since the various impedances must be matched, or an amplifier may be needed.

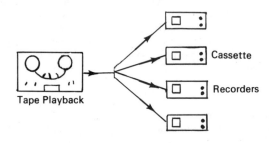

Figure 50
Simple Cassette Duplicating System

Ordinary domestic cassette recorders are not advisable for continuous duplication work. These machines are not made for continuous use, so wear may quickly be significant and cause serious difficulties.

High-speed cassette duplicators of professional quality are expensive but, on the other hand, they do a tremendous amount of work in a short time. Exact speed stability is necessary at high speed and, as signal frequencies double at double speed, the duplicators must be able to handle a wide range of frequencies.

There are a number of duplicators on the market, and most of them make several copies each time. Some duplicate onto big reels of bulk tape that later are cut up and loaded into cassettes. As an illustration of high-speed duplicators, the Telex system is pictured and explained.

182

The Telex 300 tape duplicators are high-speed systems designed for mass production of professional quality tapes by commercial, educational, institutional, or industrial facilities. The system consists of five basic components: solid state electronics, cassette master, cassette slave module, open-reel master, and open-reel slave transports.

Pictured on figure 51 is a combination that uses 4 modules—"building blocks"—and electronics. Two modules will be enough to begin the system. This basic system can be expanded by adding modules. The system can include up to 10 open-reel slaves or 6 cassette-slave modules, which will copy 18 cassettes at a time.

MODEL 300

Figure 51
Telex 300 High Speed Duplicator

The system on figure 51 consists of open-reel master, open-reel slave (not needed for cassette project), cassette master and cassette slave. This system will therefore be able to:

Copy from open-reel tape to open-reel tape.
Copy from open-reel tape to 3 cassettes.
Copy from cassette to open-reel tape.
Copy from cassette to 3 cassettes.

This system can copy about 42 C60 cassettes an hour. If 2 further slave modules are added it will be 126 C60s an hour.

Telex also manufactures a Cassette Copier, figure 52, which duplicates, in the same machine, 1 cassette from a master cassette. One further unit can be added so that 3 cassettes are copied simultaneously. The duplicating speed is 30'', so C60s are copied in less than 3 minutes. Like the 300 system, it can be delivered for either 110v or 220v, or for 60Hz or 50Hz. The cassette copier is somewhat more limited than the 300 system and further expansion is not possible. Therefore, due to its flexibility and expansion possibilities, the Telex 300 system is suggested for cassette ministries.

Figure 52
Telex Cassette Copier

For the smaller to medium-sized cassette project, Portable Recording Ministries has developed and manufactured a cassette duplicator called CD-112. The machine copies two cassettes simultaneously, but additional slave units can be added so that up to 8 copies can be made at one time. Only one track is copied at a time, but the speed is double the normal speed. The master unit is a cassette unit.

Cassettes

Small as the cassette is, you can get remarkably good sound from it. In fact, with such advances as the new tapes combined with Dolby noise-reduction circuits built into some of the newest cassette recorders, it's possible to make cassette recordings that are as good as phonograph records or tapes made on open-reel machines.

This is all the more remarkable when you consider the narrow tape that is used, and that the speed is only 1 7/8". Even on cheap cassette players a remarkable quality can be achieved.

The cassette is the only tape format that has complete compatibility between its mono and stereo versions. You can play back a mono cassette on a stereo recorder, and a stereo cassette on a mono recorder with no loss of material in either channel.

A monophonic cassette played on a stereo system will send a monophonic program from both stereo speakers. The reason for this compatibility is that the two stereo channels for the same direction are next to each other, and together take up exactly the same tape width as a monophonic track. In other tape systems, the two stereo channels for one program are separated by tracks that belong to other programs. Mono recordings frequently overlap two different program tracks resulting in gibberish on playback. This will not happen with cassettes!

Length of Cassettes

Only a limited amount of tape can be put on the small reel inside a cassette. The thinner the tape is, the more you can get in, but it is more difficult for the equipment to handle it. The number, or type, of the cassette tells how long it is. A C60 plays a total of 60 minutes, 30 minutes on each track.

Type	Total Running Time	Tape Length
C30	30 minutes (2 x 15)	150 ft.
C60	60 minutes (2 x 30)	300 ft.
C90	90 minutes (2 x 45)	450 ft.
C120	120 minutes (2 x 60)	600 ft.
C180	180 minutes (2 x 90)	900 ft.

Figure 53
Time Chart for Cassettes

Most cassettes play a couple of minutes longer on each side. The cassette ministry should not use anything longer than a C60. If the equipment is good, C90s play well; but on cheaper cassette players C90s often jam and cause difficulties. On the other hand, C60s work very well. On the mission fields almost everyone returns to C60s after trying C90s. C120 and C180 are too thin for cassette players.

Components of a Cassette

Cassettes are not all alike in quality, but they are very much alike in the parts used. The following illustrations show how a good cassette is made.

The cassette shell—made of heat resistant plastic

186

Liner sheet—chemically impregnated and silicone laminated

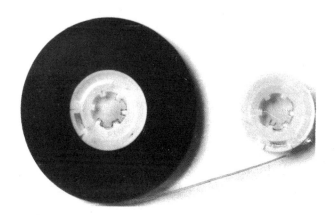

Hubs with clamps that fasten the tape

Felt pressure pad and copper spring

Antimagnetic shield plate

Guide rollers

Stainless Steel pins for rollers

Sealing screws

188

Inside the C60 cassette and the assembled product

189

An interior cassette with mismatch and a gap along the recording
edge

When tape is set in motion on this mismatched cassette, it slips
through the gap and jams, may even tear or otherwise be damaged
permanently.

Accurately matched TDK cassette

A good cassette has to be perfectly manufactured. If the shell is not properly sealed, these illustrations show what can happen.

Two tabs are located on the back side of the cassette, figure 54. These are safety tabs that will safeguard a cassette from accidental erasure. If you snap these tabs off, it automatically locks out the recording and erasure circuits of the cassette recorder.

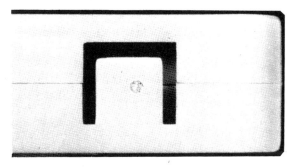

Figure 54
Safety Tab

Cassette Quality

Tape quality and reliability of cassettes are important factors. Experience shows that only good quality cassettes should be used. Any of the well-known brands are good if you use their low-noise type of cassette. Cheap cassettes are not cheap in the long run.

Difficulties and Service Tips

Even the best cassettes will occasionally cause problems, so here are some suggestions in caring for them.

1. Keep cassettes out of direct sunlight.

2. Keep cassettes in plastic bags or boxes.

3. Avoid exposing cassettes to high temperature for a long period of time. This is especially critical for thin tapes (=long cassettes).

4. Keep cassettes away from magnets and equipment, such as motors and speakers that have magnetic fields.

191

5. If the tape is loosely wound on the cassette, tighten it manually before using.

6. Don't touch the tape with your fingers.

7. Avoid too many fast rewinds.

8. After using a cassette, make sure it is tight and store it in a cool, dry place.

9. Keep recorders and players in good condition.

10. Clean heads of the cassette players often.

11. Demagnetize heads of recorders and players regularly.

Repairing or Splicing Cassette Tapes

In spite of all precautions, the tapes may still stall, jam, break, stretch, tangle, or come out of the cassette housing all together. (The Yao people in North Thailand say the intestines are coming out!!) What to do then?

Sometimes the broken ends of the tape are inside the cassette. In a case like this, you can only get at them by opening up the cassette. You'll need a miniature Philips head screwdriver, tweezers, a steady hand, and a lot of patience—but it can be done.

If the cassette is glued or welded together, the situation may still be salvageable. Crack the cassette halves apart carefully. You may not be able to use that cassette housing again, so carefully and with painstaking slowness, transfer the tape into the body of another cassette. This sort of repair can be accomplished and, indeed, has been done.

A repair of this sort can also be used if the internal mechanism of an inferior cassette becomes permanently jammed without tape breakage. The tape contents can be transferred to a good cassette case.

If the tape has broken, you can splice it together. This is done by drawing the two severed ends toward you gently, out of the cassette body, then lining them up carefully. It is best to use a tape splicing block to keep the tape properly aligned because misalignment, not visible to the naked eye, can cause jamming and breakage again.

Special splicing tape is best. It should be applied to the side of the tape that does *not* make contact with the recorder head during use, usually the shiny side which faces the inside of the cassette.

Usually the broken tape ends are so badly mangled that they cannot be aligned. In this case, align the tape ends so they overlap, and make a 45⁰ cut through the overlapping portions with a razor blade. A splicing block is useful here. Keep the overlap as small as possible to minimize the loss of recorded material. The tape ends are then carefully aligned and mended with the splicing tape. The splice is not completed until the ends of the splicing tape are trimmed off so that none extends beyond the edges of the recording tape. After the repair is completed, the excess tape should be drawn back into the body of the cassette. Winding the hub may be accomplished with a pencil inserted in the opening of the cassette shell for one of the hubs on which the tape is spooled.

CASSETTE PLAYERS
Why Use Players?

There are several reasons why cassette players are used instead of cassette recorders. A player can only play back, which is all that is necessary.

The cassette player is inexpensive.
The cassette player is easy to operate.
The cassette player cannot erase cassettes.
The cassette player does not break down easily.
The cassette player is easy to service.

Types of Players

The problem is that only a few companies manufacture cassette players, as the general market prefers cassette recorders. But there are a few models on the market. The most used are Philips (Norelco) and Hitachi.

These two makes are similar in many ways, such as size, price, and specifications. One difference is that the Philips player uses 9v (6 batteries), while the Hitachi uses 6v (4 batteries). This should make the Philips a little cheaper to use, because the more batteries used the longer they last. Most mission field experience has been with Philips N2200, the earlier model. A recent study indicates that the most available model around the world is Philips.

193

HITACHI
Solid State Portable
Cassette Tape Player
MODEL TPQ-200

FEATURES :

■ Gorgeous sounds flow from small CASSETTE with one-touch operation. ■ Unusually small size and lightweight, with convenient handle for carrying everywhere. ■ Simply operated with one hand, usable under all conditions. ■ Automatic tape-end stop system provided. ■ Convenient rewinding device is built in.

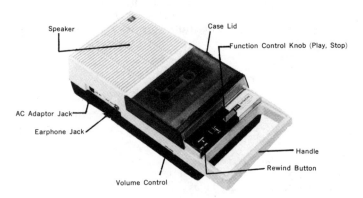

Speaker

Case Lid

Function Control Knob (Play, Stop)

AC Adaptor Jack

Earphone Jack

Handle

Rewind Button

Volume Control

SPECIFICATIONS :

Cartridge	Compact cassette
Transistor	2SB75X1 2SC458X2 2SB156X2
Thermistor	D-1EX2
Power Supply	Battery 6 V (4 "C" cells or equivalents)
Track System	Monaural double-track
Tape speed	1 ⅞ ips (3 ¾ cm/sec)
Output Power	500 mW max.
Frequency Response	100 ∼ 7,000 Hz
Speaker Size	3" (7.7 cm)
Jacks	Output. . . .1
	Ac adaptor jack. . . .1
Dimensions	Width 4 ¾" (121 mm)
	Depth 2 ½" (63 mm)
	Height 10 ¼" (262 mm)
Weight	2.8 lbs (1.3 kg)

Norelco Carry Player 1100

Norelco introduces the Carry Player 1100—the 1972 edition of the most wanted cassette player on the market! Now available with *Fast Rewind*, as well as Fast Forward, for convenient operation!

The Norelco Carry Player has been a solid hit with consumers, educators, and businessmen. Teens love it for its carry-anywhere convenience and superb sound quality. Educators choose the Carry Player for its ruggedness and reliability. Businesses choose the Carry Player for its impact in cost-efficient sales communication and training programs.

The new Norelco Carry Player 1100 features a sleek, new space-age design for easy handling and *more* eye catching sales appeal. All the famous Carry Player features are here—including "one-hand" operation and truly outstanding sound quality.

Features

- ☐ Solid state instant play
- ☐ Transistor regulated motor for accurate tape speed
- ☐ AC adaptable
- ☐ Efficient single switch operation for "Play," "Stop," "Fast Forward" and "Rewind"
- ☐ High efficiency loudspeaker
- ☐ Frequency response from 150 to 7000 Hz
- ☐ Slim, compact—measures only 10"x6¼"x2½"
- ☐ Lightweight—only 2½ lbs. with batteries
- ☐ Outlet for earphone (EP22) or extension speaker (Model 20) and AC Adapter (BE22) optional accessories

Technical Specifications

Number of tracks	Two (mono)
Tape speed	1⅞ ips
Signal-to-noise ratio	Better than —45 db
Output facilities	Earphone, AC Adapter
Output power	625 mw ± 1 db
Battery life	Approx. 16 hrs. (2 hrs/day)

How to Choose?

There are two main questions to ask: Which model is available? Which model can be serviced in the country? This last question is the most crucial factor in the decision. It may be necessary to import it or get a company to import it.

Batteries

Both players mentioned above operate on 1 1/2 volt "C" cells. Philips says that one set of 6 batteries will give 16 hours of playing time (2 hours a day). A test at Voice of Peace in Thailand gave 7 hours of continuous playing on good batteries, but after "rest times" a total of 8 more hours were gained. When used only 2 hours a day they last longer.

The bigger flashlight batteries, "D" cells, are also 1 1/2 volt each, and they ususally cost the same as "C" cells. Another test at Voice of Peace, using the same brand of batteries as above but with "D" cells, gave almost four times longer battery life. Special outside battery containers have therefore been constructed and used with almost all cassette players in Thailand (figure 55).

The advantages of outside containers are:

1. They cut battery expenses drastically.
2. "D" cells are available everywhere.
3. In the tropics all batteries can leak. Having batteries outside saves the player from damage caused by erosion.

If the cassette player is used in towns or in hospitals where electricity is available, external AC adaptors can be used.

General Maintenance of Cassette Players

A few simple rules will help to keep the cassette players running during hundreds of hours of trouble-free use. Most of these factors can be readily performed by anybody.

1. *If not in use, keep the cassette player in a plastic bag.* As far as possible the player should be kept free from dust and dirt, excessive moisture, and wide temperature extremes. Accumulated dust and dirt can degrade performance and quality, and can physically damage certain components. A plastic bag can take care of much of this.

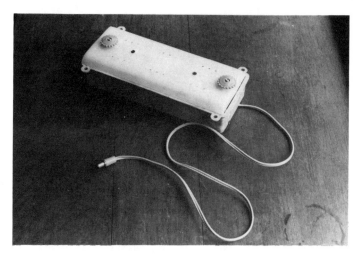

Figure 55
Outside Battery Container

2. *Clean tape head, capstan, roller and tape guides.*
When a cassette is being played, tape oxide may accumulate particularly on the tape head. (What happens to the tape head is discussed in the section on maintenance of production equipment.)

The easiest way is to use a special head cleaner cassette that has to be played only a few minutes. This cleans and polishes the head. There are a couple of problems, though. A head cleaner cassette has to be used often to be effective, and it cannot take care of really dirty heads. It does not clean capstand and roller either. It is also expensive and not readily available everywhere. If used properly and regularly, it is superior over other methods, for it will not cause misalignments or scratches on the head.

Various spray lubricants are also available for cleaning heads and other parts.

The most widely used head cleaner is alcohol. By using a cotton tip (Q-tips), the head can be rubbed lightly until all trace of dark brown deposit is removed. Tape guides and captstan can be cleaned the same way and, if ethyl alcohol is used, also the rubber roller.

197

3. *Don't run batteries too low.* When the batteries get so low that speed and sound are too slow, then change all the batteries—not just one or two. Dead batteries are hard on the motor and may corrode in the player.

4. *Teach the user how to handle and care for the player.* A few minutes of teaching may take care of many potential problems. Teach the user how to use the player, how to clean the head, how to store it when not in use, and how and when to change batteries. One mission that works with a tribal group saw most of their service problems solved when they started to give an hour's course to each new user of the cassette player.

5. *Supply cleaning kit to the user.* It is not enough to teach him how to clean the head. Supply a set of alcohol and Q-tips with each player, so that it will be available when needed. Experience shows that this is the only way to keep tape heads clean. Also supply a plastic bag!

6. *Supply service kit to area supervisor.* The missionary or pastor looking after a number of cassette players should have a simple service kit, or somebody close by who has one. The kit should contain cleaning materials, screwdrivers, small pliers, inspection mirror, brush, soldering iron, solder, head demagnetizer, alignment cassette, spares of drivebelts, plugs and wires, a small multimeter, splicing block, and splicing tape.

7. *Have reliable service facility available.* The above mentioned points should take care of most problems, but for more serious problems, a technician is needed. Arrangements should be made for such service, perhaps at the production center or a reliable secular service center. There should also be technical advice available. It is also advisable to give the players periodic servicing, which would include lubrication, brake readjustment and inside cleaning.

Technical Problems Experienced with Cassette Players

Cassette players have generally proved very reliable in spite of the conditions they work under, but it is very important that the operators of cassette ministries have service facilities available. Nobody likes to invest in equipment that cannot be serviced.

In the following list, some of the more common difficulties are given first.

1. *Dirty heads.* This is the most common cause for bad sound, but the problem exists for all equipment that uses tape. The problem is accentuated if low quality, cheap cassettes are used. When head get dirty, fidelity and volume decreases, and eventually the sound disappears.

Suggestions: Use only good quality tapes. Teach users to clean tape heads regularly. If cleaning is done often, a cleaning cassette may be used, otherwise clean as already explained. Remember that only wooden sticks, and no metal rods be used for head cleaning.

2. *Battery connections broken.* Outside battery packs are connected to the cassette player by a wire and plug. The wire can come off in the plug. The flex can break and shorten the wire. Dead corroding batteries may have spoiled the contacts in the pack.

Suggestions: Use thin wire, maybe even thin microphone wire as connection. Solder carefully. Clean contacts in the battery pack thoroughly with fine sandpaper.

3. *Batteries put in wrong.* Cassette players do not have the protection features of most other transistor equipment, so if the batteries are put in wrong, they may ruin one of the transistors and burn out the resistor.

Suggestions: The problem may be reduced by adjusting the contacts in the battery pack, but even then wires can be switched. Eliminate the problem by soldering a diode into the circuit inside the player. One diode will protect the cassette player. If four diodes are wired in as a "bridge," batteries can be put in any way and the player still operates.

4. *Cockroaches!* One missionary found eight cockroaches in the motor assembly—no wonder the drive belt was forced off! Cockroaches also eat insulation on wires and make a general mess in the player.

Suggestions: Clean out thoroughly if they get in. Remember, keep the player in a plastic bag when not in use—to keep the cockroaches out!

5. *Drive belts loose.* It happens, especially in hot and humid climates, that drive belts get slack and too long.

Suggestions: Keep a supply of spare drive belts.

6. *Connecting wire on tape head broken.* A fine coaxial wire connects the tape head with the amplifier. Due to

199

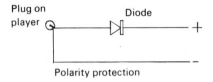

Polarity protection

Can also be placed on negative lead but with polarity turned around.

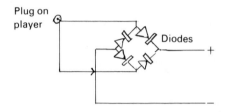

Figure 56
Bridge Circuit

the mechanical movement of the head when switching the cassette player on an off, this wire sometimes breaks or is shortened.

Suggestions: Solder the wire back on very carefully.

7. *Head out of alignment.* Misaligned tape heads cause loss of fidelity and volume. This problem is usually caused by rubbing the head too hard when cleaning it.

Suggestions: A special alignment cassette should be used, the head can then be adjusted to obtain best output.

8. *Motor gone.* Rarely does the motor itself break down, but it can happen.

Suggestion: If many cassette players are in use, always keep a spare motor ready. Wires have to be soldered off and on.

9. *Case broken.* If a cassette player is dropped badly, the sturdy case may break, though this does not usually happen.

Suggestion: If the case breaks, there is usually no other answer but to move the whole "inside" over into another case. Sometimes good glue, made for that kind of plastic material, can salvage the case. Another suggestion is to use parts from badly broken players as spare parts. It should be remembered that when a player breaks down it is always best to take it to a technician.

CHAPTER 9

Purchasing Equipment

DECIDING WHAT EQUIPMENT
TO PURCHASE

The preceding chapter on equipment use did not give advice concerning which brand, model, or make to buy. It is difficult to give blanket recommendations. In order to give valuable recommendations, certain facts have to be known. This section will, therefore, attempt to raise these questions and show how important it is that decisions are based on these factors.

Scope of the Projected Ministry

The first questions to ask concern the intended use of the equipment. How much work is projected? Which parts of the total cassette ministry are you going to perform? Will there be need for a complete setup with full facilities for production and duplication, or will a basic recording unit be sufficient? How many cassette players do you expect will be needed? Will the work operate on an intermission basis? What additional equipment would then be needed? Following the guidelines given in the previous chapter, write down specific and detailed answers to these questions in order to see what your equipment need is now and what it will be during the next few years.

Availability of Equipment and Services

The second question is a survey of possible supply. Which companies have reliable sales and service facilities? What range of equipment do they carry? All equipment will need service occasionally, so select the equipment that can be serviced, rather than equipment without service available.

Experiences Available

If you are new in the field and have no experience, seek advice from others. Radio stations have much experience with various types of equipment, and commercial companies can also give valuable advice. Operators of cassette ministries in other places may also be consulted. Base your decisions on your needs, on the equipment and service available, and on a careful evaluation of the experience of others.

PURCHASING EQUIPMENT LOCALLY

This point is mainly relevant for mission field situations. The question often comes up, Should I import equipment or buy it locally? There are a number of questions to answer first, and then the advantages of buying locally must be weighed against the advantages/disadvantages of buying from abroad.

Most Practical for Large Purchases

In large cassette projects, the number of cassettes and players needed make large purchases necessary. In the final analysis, it is more practical to buy such things locally if possible.

Immediate Delivery

Ordering from abroad may involve months from time of order to the delivery of the equipment. If you supply cassette players to several different groups, this may cause serious difficulties. Local purchasing may, on the other hand, mean delivery within a few days, or even the same day. This will make it possible for you to carry a smaller stock and not have large sums of money tied up in stock for several months.

Regularity of Supply

Ordering from abroad is usually irregular in time. Regularity of supply for cassettes and players is important, so purchase locally if the company keeps good supply in stock.

Service Is Available

Local service facilities are more important for the production equipment. When equipment is bought from a local company, they are more prepared to help with service and spare parts. Usually they only carry spare parts for equipment sold locally.

The Price Is Final

A price quoted by a local firm will be final and include all charges. On imports there will be freight, freight insurance, bank charges, duty, and import expenses, as well as time to clear the equipment through customs. In many countries these expenses will total more than the original price of the equipment. With local purchases, a few months of credit may also be available, but equipment ordered from abroad usually needs to be pre-paid.

PURCHASE FROM ABROAD

In spite of the points raised above, it may be desirable to purchase at least some of the production equipment from abroad. In some cases everything has to be imported.

Why Purchase from Abroad?

The cassette ministry requires certain prices of specialized equipment, such as duplicators, that may not be available locally. Purchasing abroad makes it possible to select exactly the type and brand of equipment needed. In a number of countries local agents carry neither professional equipment nor cassette players, so import is a necessity. It is possible, though, to get local agents to import if the order is big enough. Many problems can be avoided that way.

Where to Purchase Abroad

Purchases can be made directly from some companies, but it is usually easier to buy via one of the Christian organizations specializing in this ministry. A complete listing of such agencies is not possible, so only some of them are listed below to illustrate the type of ministries available:

Missionary Services, Inc. (Affiliated with MAP)
327 Gunderson Drive (P.O. Box 853)
Carol Stream, Illinois 60187
U.S.A.
(Formerly Missionary Equipment Service)
A wide variety of equipment is available at discount prices. Recording equipment is mainly of the domestic type. Catalogue issued annually.

Portable Recording Ministries, Inc.
681 Windcrest Dr.
Holland, Michigan 49423
U.S.A.
This agency specializes, as the name indicates, in recording equipment for Christian outreach. They have equipment for all aspects of the cassette ministry. Catalogue is available; equipment is sold at discount prices.

Bethany Fellowship, Inc.
6820 Auto Club Road
Minneapolis, Minnesota 55438
U.S.A.
Bethany Fellowship has a number of different types of equipment available at discount prices, including cassette recorders, players, and cassettes. They are agents for Hitachi and the Telex duplicators.

Gospel Recordings, Inc.
122 Glendale Blvd.
Los Angeles, California 90026
U.S.A.
110 Herring Road
Eastwood, N.S.W. 2122
Australia

Gospel Recordings have cassette players available at discount prices. Cassettes with G.R. material are available free.

Are Service and Spare Parts Available?

Some agencies may give you good prices, but their post-purchase service is poor. Find out if the equipment can be serviced locally. If not, what kind of service does the agency offer you? Is it satisfactory? Some have waited up to ten months before spare parts arrived! It would be great, of course, if some of the agencies could make the servicing of professional equipment available on the fields.

Is Postal Service Reliable?

If the ministry will be relying on supply from abroad, what are the best and most reliable supply channels? The answer may be freight by ship, postal service, or air freight. It is not advisable to rely on irregular channels.

Customs Regulations

This not only concerns the actual charge you have to pay—often 50%-80%—but also other expenses involved. Will someone have to travel 500 miles and spend 3-5 days to clear freight through customs? The total cost may then be very high indeed.

In conclusion, stay with one line or type of equipment if possible. After trying a number of different brands at Voice of Peace, the most reliable service and supply was experienced from the Philips (Norelco) company. The result is that all equipment, apart from the high-speed cassette duplicator, is gradually being replaced with Philips equipment. In this way a limited supply of spare parts is needed, the staff gets used to the equipment and its servicing, and we are saved a lot of import difficulties and work.

CHAPTER 10

Reading and Training Programs for Cassette Ministry Personnel

The use of cassettes involves people, and the principles set forth in this handbook require people to carry them out. Such personnel usually need training.

PERSONNEL NEEDED FOR THE CASSETTE MINISTRY

A cassette ministry can greatly expand the work of a church or mission, for it not only saves time, but also makes time more effective for the individual missionary or Christian worker. People are needed to operate the cassette ministry, but by looking at the need in perspective and approaching it from a well-planned angle, no additional personnel may be needed. This subject is treated from a "total project" point of view in this chapter, so it includes all the areas of a cassette ministry.

Cassette Project Supervisor

Whether or not he is called director, 'key-man,' or leader, the supervisor has overall leadership of the cassette ministry. It is important that the church or mission entering into a cassette ministry give such a person enough time to be able to do an effective job. He may also be doing most of the other jobs listed below.

Researcher

Since the work must be based on research data, including overall strategy and planning as well as programming, somebody must be available for this aspect of the ministry unless the leader can do it himself.

Technician

Any ministry using electronic equipment must have personnel to operate that equipment. The missionary organizations using cassettes can train national technicians for recording and production.

Programmers

Cassette programming is an important ministry that may take a considerable amount of time if done right. This is especially so in a Lay-Leadership-Training program. Some full-time personnel may be needed if such a full program is launched.

Local Church/Mission Supervisors

In the bigger cassette projects, the overall leader will work through local supervisors. These people may be missionaries, pastors, or Christian workers who use cassettes as part of their ministry, and they will be responsible for a certain geographical area or ministry.

Supervisors for Lay-Leadership-Training
Programs

The Lay-Leadership-Training program works by the help of area supervisors, who are responsible for the individual study groups. These supervisors are usually pastors or missionaries. Since part of their work will already be lay training, the cassette ministry may save time for them.

Users of Cassettes

For the cassette user, there is really no extra time factor involved. They have been given an effective tool to use in their ministry and outreach, a tool that will not only save their time, but will improve their ministry.

OBJECTIVES AND AREAS OF
TRAINING PROGRAMS

Each person involved in the use of cassettes should understand the material in this handbook, and keep it as a reference manual. Persons involved in producing the cassette material will most likely need further training.

Cassette Project Supervisor

Objectives of training: To be able to plan, lead, and coordinate all phases of the cassette ministry.

Suggested areas of training: all aspects of cassette ministry in principle, management, communications theory, strategy, public relations, culture, media.

Researcher

Objectives of training: To be able to uncover all data needed and on that basis make strategy and programming recommendations.

Suggested areas of training: statistics and research, consumer behavior, strategy.

Technician

Objectives of training: To be able to record and produce all material needed, and to service equipment.

Suggested areas of training: recording techniques, maintenance, production.

Programmers

Objectives of training: To be able to prepare scripts for cassettes and associated material, based on research data.

Suggested areas of training: missions, Bible, culture, scriptwriting, extension teaching, programmed instruction, communications theory, use of media.

Local Church/Mission Supervisors

Objectives of training: To be able to select cassettes, organize and supervise users, and be able to service players and cassettes.

Suggested areas of training: management, evangelism, counseling, servicing, use of cassettes.

"Extension" (CBS) Supervisors

Objectives of training: To be able to guide and help local study groups so that they will learn and follow the material.

Suggested areas of training: Bible teaching, extension teaching, counseling, servicing, use of cassettes.

Users of Cassettes

Objectives of training: To be able to use cassettes in the various phases of Christian outreach.

Suggested areas of training: evangelism, use of cassettes.

Work and Training Overlap

The areas of work will overlap, and so will the training needs. In some cassette projects one man may do most of the work; in others, 30 different people may be involved. The above areas of training are, therefore, only guidelines. The following suggested reading and training will therefore be dealt with according to subjects rather than the headings above, and the reader can select the areas he needs to study or get further training in.

BIBLIOGRAPHY OF SUGGESTED READINGS

The inquisitive student can learn much by individual study if he knows what to study. The following selection of books and journals has been limited, so that it is realistic to suggest that the material be studied. There are, of course, many other excellent books on most of the subjects.

Missions

Peters, George W. *A Biblical Theology of Missions.* Chicago: Moody Bible Institute, 1972.

Wagner, Peter C. *Frontiers in Missionary Strategy.* Chicago: Moody Press, 1971.

Clark, Dennis E. *Missions in the Seventies.* London: Scripture Union Press, 1970.

Evangelical Missions Quarterly. Published by Evangelical Missions Information Service, Inc., Box 794, Wheaton, IL 60187, U.S.A.

Evangelism/Church Growth

McGavran, Donald. *Understanding Church Growth.* Grand Rapids, Michigan: William B. Eerdmans Publishing Company, 1970.

Gerber, Vergil. *A Manual for Evangelism/Church Growth.* South Pasadena, Calif.: William Carey Library, 1973.

Church Growth Bulletin. Fuller Theological Seminary, 135 N. Oakland, Pasadena, Calif. 91101.

Teaching by Extension Methods

Covell, Ralph R.; Wagner, Peter C. *An Extension Seminary Primer,* South Pasadena, Calif.: William Carey Library, 1971.

Winter, Ralph D. *Theological Education by Extension.* South Pasadena, Calif.: William Carey Library, 1969.

Culture

Nida, Eugene A. *Message and Mission.* New York: Harper and Row Publishers, 1960.

Mayers, Marvin K. *Notes on Christian Outreach in a Philippine Community*. South Pasadena, Calif.: William Carey Library, 1970.

Mayers, Marvin K. *Christianity Confronts Culture*. Grand Rapids: Zondervan, 1974.

Communications Theory

Schramm, Wilbur. *Mass Media and National Development*. Stanford, California: Stanford University Press, 1964.

Schramm, Wilbur; Roberts, Donald F. *The Process and Effects of Mass Communication*. Chicago: University of Illinois Press, 1971.

Mortensen, David C. *Communication: The Study of Human Interaction*. New York: McGraw-Hill, 1972.

Media Channels

McLuhan, Marshall. *Understanding Media*. Signet Books. New York: The New American Library, Inc., 1964.

Voelker, Francis and Ludmila. *Mass Media*. New York: Harcourt Brace Jovanovich, Inc., 1972.

Nichols, Alan. *The Communicators*. Sydney: Pilgrim Productions Limited, 1972.

Turnstall, Jeremy, ed. *Media Sociology*. Urbana: University of Illinois Press, 1970.

Consumer Behavior

Engel, James F.; Kollat, David T.; Blackwell, Roger D. *Consumer Behavior*. New York: Holt Rinehart and Winston Inc., 1973.

Statistics and Research

Klugh, Henry E. *Statistics: The Essentials for Research*. New York: John Wiley & Sons, Inc., 1970.

Boyd, Harper W. Jr.; Westfall, Ralph. *Marketing Research*. Homewood, Illinois: Richard D. Irwin, Inc., 1972.

Webb, Eugene; Campbell; Schwartz and Sechrest. *Unobtrusive Measures: non-reactive research in the Social Sciences*. Chicago: Rand McNally, 1966.

Communications Strategy

Engel, James F.; Wales, Hugh G.; Warshaw, Martin R. *Promotional *Strategy*. Homewood, Illinois: Richard D. Irwin, Inc., 1971.

Kollat, David T.; Blackwell, Roger D.; Robeson, James F. *Strategic Marketing*, New York: Holt, Rinehart and Winston, Inc., 1972.

Management (Leadership)

Alexander, John W. *Managing Our Work*. Downers Grove, Illinois: Inter-Varsity Press, 1972.

Hendrix, Olan. *Management and the Christian Worker*. Vepery, Madras: Evangelical Literature Service, 1970.

Johnson, James. *The Nine to Five Complex*. Grand Rapids: Zondervan Publishing House, 1972.

Programming

Hilliard, Robert L. *Writing for Television and Radio*, New York: Hastings House, 1967.

Mager, Robert F. *Preparing Instructional Objectives*. Belmont: Fearon Publishers, 1962.

Zimbardo, Philip; Ebbesen, Ebbe B. *Influencing Attitudes and Changing Behavior*. Reading: Addison-Wesley Publishing Company, 1970.

Programmed Texts

Ward, Ted and Margaret, *Programmed Instruction for Theological Education by Extension*. East Lansing: Cameo, 1971.

Espich, James E.; Williams, Bill. *Developing Programmed Instructional Materials*. Belmont: Fearon Publishers, 1967.

Recording Techniques

Recording for Broadcasting. Far East Broadcasting Co., Inc., Box 2041, Manila, Philippines.

Monthly Magazine *Tape*. Anglia Echo Newspapers Lts., 2-6 High Street, Haverhill, Suffolk, England.

Nisbett, Alec. *The Technique of the Sound Studio*. New York: Hastings House, 1962.

Tremaine, Howard M. *The Audio Cyclopedia* 2nd. Ed. Indianapolis: Howard W. Sams & Co.

Productions of Programs

Miltion, Ralph, *Radio Programming*. London: Geoffrey Bles, Ltd., 1968.

Oringel, Robert. *Audio Control Handbook*. New York: Hastings House, 1966.

Crews, Albert R. *Radio Production Directing*. Belmont: Wadsworth Publishing Co.

Zettle, Herbert, *Television Production Handbook*. Belmont: Wadsworth Publishing Co., Inc., 1968.

Maintenance of Equipment

Ritter, Heinz. *Tape Questions—Tape Answers*. Published by Josef-Keller-Verlag, Stansberg. Distributed by BASF Systems, Inc., Crosby Drive, Bedford, Mass. 01730.

Nortronics Recorder Care Manual, 5th ed. Nortronics Company, Inc., Recorder Care Division, 8101 Tenth Avenue North, Minneapolis, Minnesota 55427.

Service Manuals and Circuit Diagrams for individual pieces of equipment.

TRAINING PROGRAMS SUGGESTED

For the individual who wants to progress beyond private reading and learn more, there are schools, seminars, and training facilities available for communication studies. The listing below is only meant to be representative of what is available.

Schools

Wheaton Graduate School offers a Master of Arts degree with a major in communications. This innovative program includes advanced training in communications research.

Hongkong Baptist College has a communications program that is primarily geared to the Asian scene with courses in radio, television, and print, leading to a B.A. degree. *Moody Bible Institute* gives training in the use of radio at their facilities in Chicago. *Oral Roberts University* also has a communications program at the undergraduate level. This program includes training at their professional radio and television facilities.

The *International Institute of Christian Communication* is operated by Daystar Communications in Nairobi. It is a kind of extension course that mainly teaches the use of scientific research in Christian ministry through residential sessions, and field laboratory work.

Seminars

Different organizations sponsor seminars in various parts of the world. Some of these can be of great help to people involved in cassette projects.

There are seminars or workshops on Theological Education by Extension, on Programmed Instruction, and on Evangelism and Church Growth—all of which have bearing on cassette work.

Portable Recording Ministries arrange annual seminars on cassettes and recording techniques. Ken Anderson Films also conducts an annual seminar on the use of various audio visual materials.

In many countries Christian groups are working together at radio and communications seminars. This is a good way to expand staff training beyond the regular training programs. By concentrating on one or two subjects each time, a good result can be obtained by a week of instructions.

People involved in cassette ministries will, of course, want to see seminars specifically on that subject. Seminars held on a regional plan for key personnel is suggested as well as an annual seminar for local supervisors, especially those supervising Lay-Leadership-Training programs.

On-the-Job Training

A trained leader will be able to train his staff "on the job" to a certain extent, but specific training programs should definitely be outlined and followed. People planning to start cassette ministries can also profitably spend some time observing another project already in operation. Time spent at a radio studio will help the person with no recording experience.

Some commercial companies are willing to let a person work there and observe work for a month or so. This is of special interest if one type or brand of equipment is selected, so that experience in servicing that particular type of equipment can be gained.

Training institutions and other organizations should also be encouraged—and challenged—to send instructors and engineers out to various places for short term on-the-job-training. If an instructor comes in and trains the staff in their own environment, learning can be directly and immediately applied. If the staff has to go elsewhere, application may be almost impossible.

Summary

Cassettes have been on the market only a few years, but they have already proved to be very effective tools in Christian communication. As in any other media, the cassette has to be used according to its inherent advantages and programmed for specific purposes to show its full effectiveness.

When presenting the Christian Gospel in the context of a non-Christian culture, the communication process is, to a large degree, a learning process, while in the Christian culture it is more of a "choice" process. (The "de-Christianization" that is going on in the West makes the learning process necessary there, too!) Because the cassette is basically a teaching tool, it will be at its best when used for the purpose of learning.

A cassette ministry needs to be seen in the context of the total program which the Great Commission calls for. The cassette is different from radio, television, and literature. Each media can do certain things other media cannot.

In order to be able to plan, program and use cassettes, some research is needed. Such research will include spiritual segmentation of the population, research of attitudes and interests, an analysis of the cultural and social setting, analysis of media use, and information about internal resources in the form of personnel, facilities and finance. It is on the basis of this data that an effective strategy can be planned.

Organizing a cassette project includes all aspects of the ministry, but many areas of the work may be cared for by other groups. Close cooperation is, therefore, strongly adviced. Operating principles, including financial policy, need to be stated, and a distribution system established.

The purpose of the programming for the Christians is aimed at building him up in the faith and knowledge of the Scriptures; but for the new Christian, it will give him a firm foundation for his new faith and the ability to witness to relatives and friends. Further maturity and understanding of the Scriptures can also be taught by cassette.

Evangelistic use of cassettes is different from evangelistic use of radio and other mass media. The cassette will usually be used by a Christian. The main questions to ask are, How and where is the cassette going to be used? Then program it for that purpose.

The use of cassettes in lay-leadership-training has many advantages, especially among people with lesser reading capabilities. This use of cassettes has many things in common with extension teaching and programmed instruction principles, yet it also has some unique features.

The production of cassettes involves three steps: basic recordings, producing the master tape, and copying cassettes. The facilities needed for these steps do not necessarily have to be in the same place.

Problems often exist for the missionary in obtaining equipment. The decision as to which type of equipment to purchase and where to purchase it will mainly be governed by where service is available.

The person entering into a cassette project may need further training. Instruction and training is needed for all involved. Study courses are available and seminars can be arranged. A good selection of books is available on subjects related to the cassette ministry.

The cassette has tremendous possibilities for the missionary or Christian worker who uses it. As a tool, it can help to improve and enlarge a man's ministry. It will never take the place of the personal ministry, and it will not diminish the need for total reliance on the Holy Spirit and His power. May God help each one of His servants to use cassettes in the right way and to their fullest potentials.

NOTES

Chapter Two

1. Mark 16:15.

2. Matthew 28:19.

3. Matthew 28:20.

4. See "A Biblical Theology of Missions" by George W. Peters, pp. 159-198, for a good treatment of the missionary task.

5. Philippians 2:5-11.

6. 1 Corinthians 9:22.

7. Acts 16:6-7.

8. Olan Hendrix, *Management and the Christian Worker* (Vepery, Madras: Evangelical Literature Service, 1970), pp. 2-3.

9. 1 Chronicles 12:32.

10. Marshall McLuhan, *Understanding Media* (New York: McGraw-Hill Book Company, 1964).

11. 1 Corinthians 3.

12. For detailed study of the effects of mass communication the following publications are suggested: James F. Engel, David T. Kollat and Roger D. Blackwell, *Consumer Behavior* (New York: Holt, Rinehart and Winston, Inc., 1973). Wilbur Schramm, *Mass Media and National Development* (Stanford: Stanford University Press, 1964). Wilbur Schramm, Donald F. Roberts, ed. *The Process and Effects of Mass Communication* (Urbana: University of Illinois Press, 1971). Jeremy Tunstall, ed. *Media Sociology* (Urbana: University of Illinois Press, 1970). A Technical Report to the Surgeon General's Scientific Advisory Committee on *Television and Social Behavior* (Vol. 1-6). Published by U.S. Department of Health, Education and Welfare, 1972.

13. James F. Engel, David T. Kollat and Roger D. Blackwell, *Consumer Behavior* (New York: Holt, Rinehart and Winston, Inc., 1973), pp. 52-54.

14. Andrew Tudor, "Film, Communication and Content," in *Media Sociology*, ed. by Jeremy Tunstall (Urbana: University of Illinois Press, 1970), pp. 92-103.

15. Michael Gurevitch, "The Structure and Content of Television Broadcasting in Four Countries," Vol. 1 of "A Technical Report to the Surgeon General's Scientific Advisory Committee on *Television and Social Behavior*." (Published by U.S. Department of Health, Education, and Welfare, 1972), pp. 374ff.

16. Marshall McLuhan, *Understanding Media* (New York: McGraw-Hill Book Company, 1964), pp. 36-45.

17. Source: Radio Advertising Bureau, Inc., Research.

18. See page 42.

19. Some of these points are adapted from: Wilbur Schramm, *Mass Media and National Development*, pp. 127-144.

20. Engel, Kollat and Blackwell, *Consumer Behavior*, pp. 271-274. Many of the published studies concerning television effectiveness seem to be invalidated by the measurement techniques used. See also A. W. Wicker, *Attitudes vs. Actions: The Relationship of Verbal and Overt Behavioral Responses to Attitude Objects*. Journal of Social Issues, Vol. 25, 1969, pp. 41-78.

21. Erwin P. Bettinghaus, *Persuasive Communication* (New York: Holt, Rinehart, Winston, 1972), p. 169.

22. *Soon* is a bimonthly, direct-mail publication. The content is limited to testimonies and relevant articles. The follow-up materials, including a New Testament, are kept within the 1000-word vocabulary.

23. Mainly distributed by Gospel Recordings, Inc.

Chapter Three

1. Henry E. Klugh, *Statistics: The Essentials for Research* (New York: John Wiley & Sons, Inc., 1970) and Harper W. Boyd, Jr., Ralph Westfall, *Marketing Research* (Homewood, Illinois: Richard D. Irwin, Inc. 1972).

2. Matthew 13:23.

3. A stratified sample is often used in research for practical reasons. The research universe—here the non-Christian population—is divided into sub-universes, or stratas, and an equal number of interviews is obtained from each strata. The individual samples are then randomly selected within each strata.

4. A random sample is a sample in which each one in a universe has an equal chance of being selected. If such procedures are followed, the present example will, on an 18-point scale, give a precision of $\pm$ .45 at a confidence level of 95%.

5. H. P. Philips, *Thai Peasant Personality* (Berkeley: University of California Press, 1965).

6. See *Marketing Research* by Boyd and Westfall, or a similar text.

Chapter Four

1. John W. Alexander, *Managing Our Work* (Downers Grove: InterVarsity Press, 1973), p. 9. The revised edition of this work was copyrighted © 1972 by InterVarsity Christian Fellowship of the U.S.A., and the use of the quotation is by the permission of InterVarsity Press.

2. *Ibid.*, p. 14.

3. See section on inter-mission cooperation.

4. See section on pricing.

5. See section on nationalization program.

6. Marvin K. Mayers, *Christianity Confronts Culture* (Grand Rapids: Zondervan, 1974).

7. James Johnson, *The Nine to Five Comples* (Grand Rapids: Zondervan Publishing House, 1972), p. 101. This work was copyrighted © 1972 by The Zondervan Corporation, and the use of the quotation is by permission of that corporation.

8. For developing pricing policies on the basis of business principles, see Kollat, Blackwell, Robeson, *Strategic Marketing* (New York: Holt, Rinehart and Winston, Inc., 1972), pp. 252-281.

Chapter Five

1. Thai Edition: Ken Taylor, *Family Worship*.
2. Acts 17:17.

Chapter Six

1. Eugene A. Nida, *Message and Mission* (New York: Harper and Row, 1960), p. 177.

Chapter Seven

1. 2 Timothy 2:2.
2. For an interesting discussion of the nature of the church, see: Ralph R. Covell and C. Peter Wagner, *An Extension Seminary Primer* (South Pasedena: William Carey Library, 1871), pp. 15-24.
3. Ralph R. Covell and C. Peter Wagner, *An Extension Seminary Primer*, pp. 8-12. A close study of that chapter is encouraged.
4. Ralph R. Covell and C. Peter Wagner, *An Extension Seminary Primer*, pp. 30-31.
5. A major part of the Cassette Bible School work has been done by Mrs. Rosemary Charters and Mr. Wilf Overgaard.
6. Ted and Margaret Ward, *Programmed Instruction for Theological Education by Extension* (Michigan: Cameo, 1971), p. 9.
7. A research program planned for 1974/75 will also aim at a detailed analysis of the present, as well as potential, students.
8. Robert F. Mager, *Preparing Instructional Objectives* (California: Fearon Publishers, 1962).
9. It is believed that a training program on cassettes can be produced for illiterates. Some experimentation is being done.
10. Ted Ward, *Split-Rail Fence: An Analogy for the Education of Professionals* (East Lansing: Michigan State University, Learning Systems Institute, 1969).
11. Such a research program is presently being carried out at the Voice of Peace.

Chapter Eight

1. Herbert Zettl, *Television Production Handbook* (Belmont: Wadsworth Publishing Company, Inc., 1961), p. 76.